WHAT TO DO WHEN LIFE IS DRIVING YOU CRAZY™

Help for Handling Everyday Crises for the Rest of Your Life

Barbara A. Berg, M.S.W., L.C.S.W.

CREATIVE OPTIONS PUBLICATIONS

WHAT TO DO WHEN LIFE IS DRIVING YOU CRAZY™

Help for Handling Everyday Crises for the Rest of Your Life

Published by:

Creative Options Publications

2058 N. Mills Avenue, Suite 116

Claremont, CA 91711

Library of Congress Catalog Number: 96-93010
ISBN: 0-9654014-0-5

Cover production and page design by One-On-One Book Production, West Hills, California.

Disclaimer

The case histories and other descriptions in this book are composites only and do not refer to specific individuals. All names, descriptions, situations and other particulars have been substantially altered to protect the confidentiality and privacy of clients and others with whom I have worked.

This book is not intended to take the place of psychotherapy or other appropriate health care. Readers are strongly urged to consult an appropriate health care professional to determine if treatment is necessary.

The author and publisher are not affiliated with and do not endorse any of the "Suggested Resources" listed at the back of this book.

This book is sold without any warranties or guarantees of any kind, and author and publisher disclaim any liability, loss or damage caused by its contents.

Note: To eliminate the bulkiness of "he" and "she" phraseology, the use of "he" and "she" will be alternated throughout the book.

Dedication

This book is dedicated to Ronnie, my husband, who has been with me through thick and thin. I truly am thankful for his support and patience throughout the process of this book. Also, to my darling daughter, Brittany, who has sung and danced and cheered me on.

My mother deserves recognition for teaching me the great value of "being who you came here to be" and "letting no one keep you from your dreams."

This book is also dedicated to anyone who sincerely desires to experience more happiness and less stress in his life.

In this rapidly changing and challenge-filled world it is often necessary for all of us to achieve new perceptions and change our course of action to attain the satisfaction and joy we desire.

It's easy to stay stuck on a treadmill, moving but going nowhere, using the same ineffective habitual responses to people, situations and problems.

It is a brave person who is willing to look at her dilemma in a new light, and to move in a healthy new direction, one that makes life more meaningful each day and results in long-term improvement.

Acknowledgments

I owe so much to so many. I am constantly amazed how one's own belief in one's self can be so magnificently fostered by the love and support of others. I want to thank Dr. Dojelo Russell, professor emerita and past director of the Social Work Educators' Preparatory Program of the School of Social Work of Virginia Commonwealth University, for having faith in me. She was one of the first people who helped me acknowledge my strengths and develop skills in teaching as a way to help others. I also give thanks for meeting my dear friend and mentor, Alma Lerner Visser, who has consistently and patiently lit my way to a more fulfilling professional and personal life.

Judith Pillsbury, one of my dearest mentors, has been pivotal in encouraging me with this project from its inception to completion. She was instrumental in helping me find Dan Poynter who led me to Carolyn Porter, Karen Stedman, and Alan Gadney for final editing and finished production.

Thanks to Ana Collisson for her administrative help, and Pat Woy's initial editing and continual support which got this book off the ground.

I have lived through each one of these chapters to create this book. It has been a humbling privilege as a licensed clinical social worker to have the opportunity to listen to the words and hearts of my clients. Cases and stories are from altered composites of clients, people in general, as well as my own experiences together with insights and lessons I have learned.

I have greatly appreciated being associated in private practice with Denel Duprez, L.C.S.W., Jerry Duprez, Ph.D., Gina Lamphere, Ph.D. and others at Haven Psychological Associates in Rancho Cucamonga, California. Other supportive colleagues include Ginny Gibalante, L.C.S.W., who helped me during my California licensing process, and Mary Ann Teague, L.C.S.W., who supervised me when I was an intern at West End Family Counseling in Ontario, California.

It has also been a great opportunity and an inspiring experience to speak to audiences and conduct workshops and speeches throughout Southern California over the past decade, and to develop and customize Cognitive Stress Management[SM] (CSM) for both individual clients and workshop participants.

Kate Kelley, my pal, constantly reminds me of the humorous side of it all. She also advises me to live in the moment. Marsha Krohn, D.C., my dear friend from Douglass College days and Liz Roman are the best "girls' trip" travel buddies and long distance phone call friends I could ever have.

Others in my life who have helped me to take life less seriously and to find the joy in being myself, professionally and personally, are (in alphabetical order): Beverly Benjamin, Ph.D.; Linda Conrad, M.F.C.C.; Ruth Deich, Ph.D.; Leonaine Dixon, M.F.C.C.; Janet Dreyer; Serena Hicks; Susan Kemp; Janelle Killingsworth; Jane Kircher; Cindi Lane, Reiki Master; Pat Lightfoot; Allison Mori-Coe; Liz Popoff; Julie Schael; Rita Dasgupta Sherma; Mary Catherine Theal; Joann Turner, C.M.T. and Reiki Master; and Linda Wheeler, C.M.T.

About the Author

Barbara Berg holds a Master's Degree in Social Work and conducts psychotherapy and therapy counseling to children, teens, adults, couples and families. She is a mental health therapist at Haven Psychological Associates in Rancho Cucamonga. Berg is an experienced consultant holding workshops and lecturing in the areas of child care, work/family related issues, balancing life and work, communication between couples, and supervisor and employee interaction. Her presentation and workshop clients range from large manufacturing, aerospace and utility companies to schools, colleges and city employees.

Many of her workshops are based on "Cognitive Stress Management," and happiness levels. She is the author of several published articles and is the recipient of such awards as the International Who's Who of Professionals and Business Women, Who's Who Among Human Service Professionals and Who's Who Among Young American Professionals.

Married and the mother of a daughter, Barbara Berg is currently a member of the National Association of Social Workers, and an associate member of the California Association of Marriage and Family Counselors. She is also on a 3.0 United States Tennis Association amateur tennis team at the Claremont Club in Claremont, California.

TABLE OF CONTENTS

INTRODUCTION

"The real voyage of discovery consists not in seeking new landscapes but in having new eyes."

—Marcel Proust

This book, *What To Do When Life Is Driving You Crazy,* is written for you and the millions of other people who are caught up in the "fast track," where life seems more complex and confusing than ever before. More fast balls are thrown at you on a daily basis than you ever imagined possible, and when major life issues are tossed in the mix, it can all be so overwhelming!

Everyday crazy making occurs when we insist on acting and reacting to events and people the SAME way again and again, then feel hurt and disappointed when we don't get DIFFERENT results. It's truly amazing how much we resist doing things differently when there is often a more effective way available to us. We just get so attached to doing things our usual way.

Before you can understand the crazy-making thoughts in your mind, you'll need to view your personal life in the context of what's happening in the world around you. Here are some of the facts you face in today's world:

❈ Divorces are almost the norm with 50 percent of all marriages in the United States ending in divorce.

❈ So many American households are headed up by single parents who are doing the work of two people and trying to make sure their children "have it all."

❈ Job security is a thing of the past as many major companies continue to restructure and layoff thousands of people.

❈ Bankruptcy, almost unheard of until the '80s, devastates many people every year.

❈ Drive-by shootings are on the rise.

❈ Kids and adults are on street drugs in every community.

❈ AIDS is increasing around the world.

❈ Reports of incest and child pornography are proliferating.

❈ Murder and robbery are occurring all the time.

All the above, plus a multitude of other societal problems, are frightening enough to make us believe the whole world has gone crazy. When these issues are combined with your relationship, career and family problems, daily life becomes difficult.

Where does today's crazy world leave you as an individual? Is there anything you can do to keep yourself from going over the edge or from adding to the chaos around you?

While this book can't directly change the course of society, it can help you, as an individual, deal with your personal issues. It can help you become more effective in coping with the crazy-making days in your life. This book can also help you change your overwhelming negative thoughts into positive ones during stressful times.

These chapters are intended to help those who are willing to observe and make some sense of their own emotions and who are willing to explore and to increase their options. The reader will be helped to find some still waters in order to think clearly and to make wise decisions as quickly as possible before becoming further buried in everyday quicksand.

This book is designed for people who need immediate helpful steps to consider and for those who desire long-term input and guidance.

1. IMMEDIATE HELP—If you need immediate help with an overwhelming situation, you may want to start reading chapters 2, 3 and 4 now. You'll receive help on finding "still waters." These chapters will help you acquire a sense of peace from which to think clearly and make wise decisions.

2. LONG-TERM GUIDANCE—If your relationships and other aspects of your life are occasionally or always filled with crazy-making problems, this book will help you learn how to see them coming and to avoid them. It will also help you alter your part in creating problems if you notice you are in a pattern. You'll soon achieve a greater understanding of why some everyday situations make you feel crazy. You'll learn how you can reduce the craziness by bringing more happiness and serenity into your daily life. The chapters are divided as follows. Chapter 1 explains the meaning of everyday crazy making, in addition to giving you lots of examples. Chapter 2 introduces the concept of Cognitive Stress Management[SM](CSM), a system that quickly helps you to get in touch with your present feelings. Chapter 3 includes an exercise to help you confront your problems now, rather than later; and, if you are seeking professional help, chapter 4 provides some information for you to consider.

The chapters in Section II offer practical and useful advice for dealing with various types of crazy making, which include no-win situations, feelings of hurt and anger, and trying too hard to be accepted. You will also gain an understanding of why you often experience these unpleasant situations.

On the final pages you will find a list of valuable resources, such as other books to read and adjunct organizations to call.

Overall, this book will help you create a method of coping with and organizing those thoughts, issues and emotions that often flare up when life throws you a curve ball—when you are already operating on overload. This method helps you develop an inner plan for controlling your thoughts. It gives you a sense of empowerment and direction to deal effectively with life's emotion-laden moments. You'll learn how to stay on top of your issues and how to detect potentially problem-filled situations brewing below the surface.

This book is designed to help you live better each day so you can wake up happier tomorrow.

EVERYDAY CRAZY MAKING... THE INSIDE STORY

You're in emotional pain about your impending job layoff, divorce, or realization that your spouse has been having an affair. You can barely think straight. You don't see an easy way out and there doesn't appear to be a happy ending in sight. You wonder how long your agony will last; yet, you know something has to give. If these feelings go on too long, you are afraid you might truly go out of your mind.

The above describes how you might feel when you're in a crazy-making dilemma. Given a similar situation, another person might have different emotions. Someone else may explain his feelings in another way.

We would all agree, however, that our circumstances don't have to be out of the ordinary or overly dramatic to be overwhelming; sometimes various issues in our lives have a way of becoming just too much to handle.

What Is Everyday Crazy Making?

Everyday crazy making is the mental process of making difficulties in everyday life even worse than they already are. That's not to say your situation—layoff, divorce, bankruptcy, unhappy marriage, runaway teenager—isn't rough already. It's just that the decisions you make during particularly difficult times may further complicate your problems.

Some people have one problem after another, yet somehow they maintain a sense of stability and roll with the punches. Others travel on a downward spiral and don't get back up until they hit rock bottom, or they may not get back up at all. And, there are those people who have an uncanny way of sabotaging their lives and creating chaos just when all is going well.

Here are more examples of this negative mental state:

❈ *Everyday Crazy Making.* Not realizing how your perspective in a particular situation can lead you to act in a manner that actually works against you.

❋ *Everyday Crazy Making.* Finding yourself consumed with hurt feelings, anger or confusion about your personal or business relationships. Witnessing old response patterns from yourself and others when you feel up against a wall.

❋ *Everyday Crazy Making.* Uncertainty about the appropriate actions to take, along with relentless thoughts about too much to do, the rut you are in, or the hopelessness of your situation.

❋ *Everyday Crazy Making.* Knowing your life is resembling a bad soap opera, but being unable to end your role in it.

❋ *Everyday Crazy Making.* Getting out of one painful dilemma and having another one hit you square in the face.

You don't have to be "out of your mind" to experience crazy days, and your situation doesn't have to be out of the ordinary or overly dramatic. It just feels chaotic at the moment. Can you relate in some way to any of the following ten real-life crazy-making incidents?

1. You catch your husband kissing your best friend.

2. Your rebellious teenage daughter begins staying out late and her grades are dropping to D's and F's.

3. Your boss wants you to work on Saturdays, and you're already doing the workload of two people.

4. Your grown child wants to move in with you just when you had decided to sell the house.

5. You crash your car into the garage door during a rain storm.

6. The person you are madly in love with tells you he/she thinks you both should date other people.

7. You discover there's a major leak in your roof at the same time your taxes are due.

8. You left a good job because your spouse got a new, out-of-town position, then, he suddenly loses his job.

9. Your wallet is stolen.

10. After time alone with your "other half," you realize once again, you would rather be almost anywhere else, without your spouse.

The previous incidents can certainly bring major stress into your life. But, the following everyday occurrences can be the straws that break your back when you already have too much to handle. Add even one of them to your crazy-making scenario, and you may be setting yourself up for an explosion in one way or another. Take note, too, how technology has gotten into the act of making our lives "crazy."

❄ You lock your keys in the car while it's running, the car security alarm goes off by mistake and you can't get inside to shut it off.

❄ You search the house for your glasses only to find they are on top of your head.

❋ As you rush out of the house for an important appointment, you realize your wallet and your appointment book are no where in sight.

❋ You set off your own home alarm system on Sunday morning as you go out to get the paper.

❋ You're driving to work and you discover the gas tank is empty and it's miles to the next gas station.

❋ As you wait to be seated in a restaurant, several other groups who came in after you get seated before your name is called.

❋ You almost have an accident with your two children in the car because you're fumbling in your purse to find out who just paged you on your beeper.

❋ You computer crashes because it has a virus, and your reports are due tomorrow.

❋ You're anxious to settle your last item of business by fax and get out of the office, but the other person's fax line continues to be busy.

❋ Your cellular phone goes "out of range" and cuts you off in the middle of an important conversation.

❋ You're trying to reach someone at an 800 number and after going through the menu a few times, you can't get your particular questions answered; it appears you will never be able to talk to a "live" customer service rep.

Responses To Everyday Crazy Making

What happens when one more straw is added? Each person will respond in a different manner. Your mind may begin to swirl in all directions, so you can barely think straight. Someone else may become teary-eyed and collapse in a heap on the sofa, and yet another person will shout out in anger at anyone who is nearby.

When you are experiencing one more problem added to your already crazy-making experience, you may not be able to view the entire situation clearly, and think you are stuck with no options to get out. Or, you may feel everyone else is against you, out to make your life miserable. Although there may be some truth in your feelings, it's also likely you are trapped in some of your own everyday crazy-making thought mechanisms. We all have them.

While it's true other people or circumstances may invite you to feel defensive and aggravate matters, it's also true that your own thinking can create more chaos when you are extremely upset or out of control. Your mind can bounce from one thought to another, making you panicky and frantic. Just at the very moment clear thinking is required, you are all tied up in knots, trying to find a solution to a problem. It's possible at this point that you could end up creating more problems.

MARGARET CREATES HER OWN CRAZY-MAKING SCENARIO

Here is one example of how everyday crazy-making problems, if left to chance and old habits, can lead to self-defeating decisions, which set you up to make matters worse.

Margaret was at her wit's end. She was married to John, a nice, but boring, sedentary man. He spent all of his free time watching sports on cable TV or playing golf all day. They had moved to a little country town far away from anywhere she wanted to go so he could continue his career with his company, and she had given up her "job of a lifetime" because it was too far away.

As John burrowed into his new position and Margaret saw no job opportunities in sight, she felt her life had come to a dead end.

She began to focus on how John was keeping her from living in a meaningful way. Every evening before she fell asleep and every morning when she awoke, she dwelled on her lack of direction and her feeling of loneliness. She was sure she could not continue to endure the monotony and strain.

When it came to Margaret's career and goals in life, she was bright enough, but undisciplined. Although she secured a few short-term freelance jobs, she always ended up feeling at a dead end.

Unable to see her own shortcomings, she focused on all of John's inequities. And, as she became angry, so did he.

After a couple of frustrating years of facing brick walls and feeling dead inside, Margaret ran away to live in another state. She left her dull husband, certain that he was the root of all her problems.

Margaret's new path led her to a man who seemed to be her "soul mate." Having cocktails in exotic restaurants and getting wet in the rain, only added to the excitement and sense of adventure. Margaret's desire for stimulating companionship, and search for something new, led her straight into the arms of this stranger who made her feel better than her own husband did. This newfound "love" further propelled her to believe the new relationship was "good," or what a relationship should be. She concluded her husband John was "bad," and he didn't deserve her companionship.

One day, however, her soul mate hit her in the face, giving her a black eye. She had all too willingly placed herself in a compromising position, never acknowledging that she didn't know this man very well at all. She didn't see the danger signs which were in front of her all along.

Margaret's new image of herself and her life were shattered. In a panic, she ran home to John, only to find out that after months of waiting for her he was now with another woman and was no longer available to her. Shocked, overwhelmed and utterly devastated by all these events, Margaret did not know where to turn. Plopping herself on the floor of the home she once lived in, she desperately wondered how she would ever get through this mess.

Perhaps you relate to Margaret. Maybe you relate to John. Maybe you find yourself in the shoes of the stranger.

Margaret wasn't necessarily all wrong for feeling angry with John. They both had their problems, but that was just part of it. Margaret was spiraling downward so fast she was too frightened to deal with her own problems. To blame John for all that was going awry was less painful to her than realizing she was adding more conflict to the situation. Because she was unable to clearly think through her dilemma and didn't effectively seek outside help, she brought even more chaos into her life.

In the past, Margaret had been in unhappy situations, and instead of solving a particular issue, she had a habit of creating another one at the same time. Since she was responding out of habit, she didn't realize she had other choices. She also didn't realize she was stuck in a pattern.

That's the frightening part about crazy-making dilemmas. Many times they seem to come out of the blue. Quite often, however, they are the result of past troubles, old pains and unrealistic expectations that have been brewing below the surface.

Looking At Your Options

In crazy-making situations, you tend to forget you have more than one option. You may really believe you are stuck in a corner with no way out. Often, however, the most appealing or only option you think you have leads you to make the wrong decision and adds more turmoil to your life, often making it impossible to see the full picture objectively.

Of course, some crazy-making situations are more severe, overwhelming and longer lasting than others. If you are experiencing any of the following symptoms, seek help immediately:

1.   You are so consumed with anger or hurt feelings you can't think about anything else.

2. You're dizzy and disoriented and can't seem to get oriented.

3. Your heart is beating fast; you're in a panic; and you can't focus on these pages or anything else right now.

4. You can only think about ways to relieve the pain, which involves hurting yourself, someone else or both.

5. If you or someone else is in immediate danger, call 911.

What To Do When Life Is Driving You Crazy gives you insights and perspectives to help you respond to situations so your life becomes smoother, somewhat easier and less chaotic. You'll learn to detect the warning signs ahead and enjoy life's moments more along the way.

Now, let's get going.

FIRST THINGS FIRST: COGNITIVE STRESS MANAGEMENT

WHAT'S YOUR STRESS LEVEL?
HOW DO YOU FEEL ABOUT LIFE RIGHT NOW?

You can check your own stress level right now, as you may be in the middle of a crazy-making situation and not fully realize it. You could be experiencing a lot of stress and you may feel you are handling it quite well. However, you may be getting to the point where the situation could get out of control. There are times in life when it is hard to determine if you can tackle what life has handed you, or if you are getting in way over your head.

Stress can be defined in many ways. However, for the purposes of getting a grip on your present situation, think of your dilemma as fitting into three basic categories—circuit overload, conflicting goals or being hit by a bomb. Quite often, your problem may fit into more than one of these categories.

Note: This chapter will help you focus on the type of stress you are experiencing and help you access how much stress is in your life. Chapter 3 and beyond, will help you go into more depth about the kinds of steps you can take to deal with your issues.

It's critical right now to sort out what is important for you to do without adding additional emotions and feelings of guilt. During stressful times, don't dwell on worrying about what others will think. Your own well-being is at stake, and you won't be any good to anyone if you are not good to yourself.

Circuit Overload

You are being pulled in all directions, overwhelmed by many different demands. The pressure is so great you feel you will explode if one more thing gets dropped in your lap. Maybe you have already exploded and now you feel as though you will collapse.

Here are some specific examples of circuit overload:

❃ The Halloween play for your third-grade class starts in two hours. Some of the students don't have their costumes, and the main characters don't really know their lines. Their parents will be attending, and as the new teacher, you want to show them your best. Meanwhile, your hospitalized mother keeps calling on the phone, and the principal wants to talk to you about how disruptive her calls have been to the school secretary.

❋ Despite the fact you are working a 50-hour week, the bills never diminish. Now, your 3-year old car needs a major overhaul, and your savings account is nil.

❋ As a single working parent, you struggled to make ends meet and had some free time to enjoy your two children. Now, after you've taken on a second job to buy the Christmas presents they want, you find out they're becoming discipline problems at the day care center.

How To Deal With Circuit Overload

Make a list of everything that requires your attention. Once you have completed the list, go back and cross out the requests and demands that can be put on hold for a week or two. Who knows, maybe you will find a couple of demands you can completely let go. This is no time to let your self-critical instincts govern what you should do. You are doing the best you can. Even if everything isn't just-so, keep in mind that your well being is at stake. Leave the little things for later...or never. And, don't give any task more energy than it deserves.

This is the time to let people know you have gone beyond your limit, even if you've never recognized or told others you have a limit.

It's time to use the word "NO," to be less of a perfectionist, and to delegate your work to others, if possible.

Chances are people won't be pleased to hear you are less available to them, especially your children. Some people may even think you've abandoned ship. However, you may be entertaining misconceptions about what others want from you.

Conflicting Goals

You are faced with conflicting goals that are emotionally tearing you apart. You are uncertain about what direction you should take.

Here are two examples of conflicting goals:

❋ A relative who is low on funds has moved in with you. Because you genuinely care about this person, you want to help out as best as you can. However, the rest of your household is complaining about the inconvenience and this relative's cantankerous personality. You want to provide your family with a comfortable living arrangement, yet, help your relative and maintain peace of mind for yourself. All three goals cannot be achieved simultaneously.

❋ Because you drive two hours to your high-powered job, it takes away time you want to spend with your new twin girls. You like your job and love your home. If you moved closer to work, you couldn't afford a home as attractive as the one you have now. You feel torn and stressed. Fights between you and your spouse are all too commonplace, and both of you can't seem to agree if it's a good idea for her to get a job right now.

How To Deal With Conflicting Goals

Write them down. Maybe there is more involved in the situation than you realize. The simple act of writing down your thoughts and feelings helps you to view them more objectively. Perhaps you can then see your conflicting goals as problems to be solved rather than monsters who will defeat or destroy you.

Being Hit By A "Bomb"

Although it is normal for pressures and complications to arise unexpectedly during your lifetime, some crises can throw you for a real loop.

Here are some examples of bombs:

❉ Having a loved one die.

❉ Finding out dad isn't your father.

❉ Discovering that your spouse is having an affair and wants out of the marriage.

❉ Experiencing violence such as rape.

❉ Getting hurt when you total your new car.

❉ Getting fired.

❉ Losing your home in a tornado or another type of disaster.

Although some bombs are more devastating than others, they all disturb your mental stability and lower your resistance to physical illness. And extraordinary problems unfortunately have a way of hitting when you are already overloaded with stress. They make it next to impossible for you to decide what to do next.

No two people respond to traumatic or stressful incidents in the same way. When incidents burst into your life you may respond immediately. Or, you may suppress your feelings, but if you do they will creep up slowly often taking months or even years to surface; and then you may explode in ways you never would have expected.

What To Do If You've Been Hit By A Bomb

First, don't make any hasty decisions. Seek out someone to assist you, such as a counselor who can help you understand the options available to you at this time.

If you are thinking, "I just don't want to be a burden," take these words out of your vocabulary. This is the time to seek your safest and most understanding friend, family member, spiritual or religious leader or recommended professional.

These are times when you may feel your life will never be the same again. When dramatic changes are occurring, acknowledge and then accept them, but at your own pace. It's no time to make rash decisions. Life isn't out to "get" you, even though it can seem that way. Don't force yourself to think *you* have to be overly strong through the whole thing. Let people be there for you and help you through. You deserve comfort and love.

These, then, are the three basic categories of stressful situations: circuit overload, conflicting goals, being hit by a bomb. If you are involved in any of these stressors, you could easily fall into a crazy-making state if you don't have a system to help you through. If you try to make too many changes too quickly, you may lead yourself into crazy-making behavior which will make the situation worse.

Of course, if your physical well being or the life of someone in your family is truly at stake, you need to make some fast moves. Quickly explore the various options you have through professional help or with those who have mastered similar situations.

(Should you be in a life-threatening situation, call 911. It is a good idea to collect phone numbers of crisis hotlines, medical professionals and hospitals ahead of time.)

Happiness Quotient

Your happiness is something that needs to be considered. Even while you are experiencing confusion and stress, there are levels of happiness and peace of mind to hold onto as your goal or standard. In fact, you could experience these levels even in the midst of your angst. Strive to keep happiness as your beacon; it's easy to forget which way is up when everything seems so down.

Let's talk about the idea of a "happiness quotient." Your happiness quotient is the amount of joy and well being you are able to draw on to sustain and to maintain in your life. Some people enjoy happiness for long lengths of time, no matter what is going on in their lives. Those who have a tendency to focus on what could go wrong, may only express joy for a few moments before plummeting into despair.

At the heart of the quotient is how much happiness you feel is available for you in this world, and deep down how much you feel you really deserve, despite what you may continually tell yourself and others.

The CSM rating scale is designed to help you consider any aspect of your life, and decide where you would place yourself in terms of how you are dealing with issues at this or any time.

The higher on the scale you are, the happier or more positive you feel about your circumstances. If you rate yourself on the low end of the scale, the more negatively stressed you are. This may be an indication that you are willing to settle for less happiness than others. You may not be taking opportunities as they come along, or you may not be exerting effort to make effective and necessary changes in improving your overall life. You may find yourself saying, "Why bother. Things won't really get better no matter what I do." Or, "Other people have worse problems. I should feel lucky things aren't that bad."

Without realizing it, you may be creating or prolonging situations that keep you stuck on a negative treadmill. Then you believe that you are always being victimized by others, which, in turn, proves that your life is more rotten than other people's lives.

Getting A New Perspective On Your Life

Take a good look inside. Are you stuck in a mode where you subtly buy into the notion that others are able to be happy, but you can never get any more joy, satisfaction and stability than you have at this time? Are you willing to accept a life of continuous upheaval because you are powerless to make changes or decisions? Do you feel what you have now is all that life has to offer you? When life is going smoothly, do you get bored easily?

If you answer yes to these questions, take a few minutes and go through the following exercise. First consider what you would like to say about yourself at the end of your life. Perhaps by looking backward, you can better aim your life toward what you envision.

Picture yourself now as though you are 95-years-old. As you reach the last months of your life, you are hopefully basking in the happiness of having had a full and satisfying existence. What would the *a* major newspaper say about you if you were featured.

Take a moment to write down your own story, what you've accomplished, achieved, etc. The more your present life reflects your newspaper story, the more likely you have a relatively high happiness quotient. The further away your life is from what you wrote, the more likely you are unhappy and have some major changes to make.

Cognitve Stress Management Rating Scale

Reading through the following Cognitive Stress Management (CSM) Scale, try to see your present level of negative stress and well being; also be aware of where you are with your happiness quotient. Take note of exactly how far you can descend on the scale before your pain makes you aware that you must either alter your point of view or take action to create change.

Rather than settling for less, consider the idea of settling for

COGNITIVE STRESS MANAGEMENT SCALE
AT A GLANCE

10. Truly wonderful. Almosts too good to be true at times, but it really is more about attitude than what is actually going on in your life.

9. Almost a 10. There is a small flaw in an issue in your life, but you can easily handle it.

8. Good. No complaints, not yet. However, you may feel that if you do not keep focused, something could throw you off course.

7. Not bad. This spot on the scale is tolerable.

6. This is not a good place to be. Time to face issues before they get worse.

5. Something has to give. Look at your options.

4. Depression and/or anxiety are taking over. Take action now before you loose energy.

3. You are probably losing sleep. Ask for help.

2. A "crisis" is looming. Remember with crisis comes opportunity. Major changes are necessary soon.

1. You're at the bottom line. Remember, when things get too bad, you have more options than you realize. Don't go down with the ship.

more. It's really a matter of deciding how much energy and effort you are willing to invest in your happiness. Consider what you said about yourself in the above exercise. Maybe it can serve as a standard for what you want your life to be.

If you are ready, use the following Cognitive Stress Management Rating Scale to check your present state of mind. The idea of managing and balancing your life begins first with finding and acknowledging how you honestly view life at this moment, and second, how you truly would like it to be.

Where are you on a scale of 1 to 10?

A number 10 means you are in great shape; a number 1 means you are hurting terribly. One complication in life, however, is that occasionally, you may be a 10 when you wake up and a 2 by mid-afternoon. Everyone has his or her own pattern. Be aware of yours, and think about what is taking place in your life at each number. You may need to arrive at an average figure if your life fluctuates from one number to another.

Read on. The pages ahead will help you in your search to find the answers that work for you. For each number on the scale, everyone has his or her own set of pictures or ideas. Retain these individual perceptions to use on your life journey to keep everyday craziness out of your life as much as possible.

Life for you is:

10. EXCELLENT. If you are a 10, you can enjoy what is going on in your life most of the time. You understand that you are at this number more because of your attitude than what is actually occurring. This means you are able to stay in a positive frame of mind without blocking out what you don't want to see.

If an issue comes along, you view it as a challenge to overcome and learn from, rather than a problem that could ruin your life. In your particular frame of mind, you are able to consider your options and make your decisions with a minimum of angst and heartache.

In fact, you have a genuine zest for life and a sincere, positive viewpoint that makes others enjoy your company. You aren't preoccupied with fear and worry. You satisfy your needs without being thoughtless and self-centered. You have a high regard for other people's feelings and needs. You are generous, but you don't give excessively, and you don't resent people when they can't meet your expectations.

As a 10, you have a comfortable sense of well being in just about all areas of your life, at least at this moment. You may not have all the answers, but you know that they will come in time.

You feel positive about yourself, what you are doing, and where you are going. Your life doesn't have to be perfect. In fact, you can experience overall joy and peace even if everything isn't exactly in the proper place. Rather, you fully acknowledge your approval of the direction you are moving in, and you have the decision-making skills to make changes as necessary and to ask for help as needed.

You are also able to look at your past in such a way that it doesn't hold you up or hinder your progress. You're not looking at life through rose-colored glasses; instead, you have a clear idea of what you have learned from an experience, what you feel you might have lost or never really had in the first place, and what you have gained. You approach people and experiences with a sense of freshness—you're not constantly triggered by old losses, pain or emptiness; and you don't generally blame others if any unhappiness comes into your life.

9. VERY GOOD. While you recognize that life is less than perfect and you've had some disappointments, you experience joy and happiness most of the time. You would like some things to be different, but you know you have always ultimately been able to handle them with help as needed. You generally like the challenges life brings you. When you don't, you are able to meet them effectively and proactively rather than reactively and feeling victimized. You have the ability to make good decisions.

As a 9, your health and energy levels are usually good, and you can accept yourself as you are most of the time. You know you have a 9 mentality when you realize that certain periods in life may bring one dilemma after another, but you don't have to succumb to them and get bogged down in depression and inactivity.

8. GOOD. You are at a place on the scale which would be comfortable for many people. You recognize that you are generally doing well. Issues and stressors can still be isolated and dealt with as minor problems rather than major setbacks.

As an 8, you recognize the importance of keeping your eyes open, because something could appear on the horizon to throw you off balance. At this point on the scale, while striving not to slip lower, you can maintain genuine happiness. You are a realist who is well aware of your human flaws and those of others. You are also open to learning more aspects of yourself that you may not yet be aware of. As you plan ahead, you are careful to not over-commit yourself, because you might have had a tendency to do so in the past. You tackle something nagging at you as soon as you can because you understand you will be better off in the long run.

You know your needs can usually be met by asserting your position with good humor. Generally, you are positive, and also you may be diplomatic when the need rises.

7. TOLERABLE. You may or may not feel satisfactory at this level. It depends on how much positive energy you are putting into your life now and what you expect of the future. You might be telling yourself, "Things could be better, but they could be worse." And, you are absolutely right.

As a 7, you have sufficient energy most of the time. You realize you have the opportunity to improve your situation in some way. However, you may be inclined to settle in and to rationalize with such statements as, "At least I have it better than most people."

Stressors are anything contributing to the aggravation of your daily life. Perhaps you are sensing some sort of underlying feeling of unease as you go about your day. Or, there may be an issue that is bothering you and you are trying to decide if you should do anything about it. Stressors can nag you into taking action. They can serve as wake-up calls, providing you with the motivation to make a change.

What To Do If You're At Level 7

Be aware of your true motivations. Are you about to marry someone who demeans you, because you are afraid to live alone? Are you avoiding looking for another job, even though your boss is unbearable, because your present job pays well and you get great benefits? It's amazing how much stress you may be willing to endure to avoid making changes in your life. It is also amazing how little you may believe life has in store for you. If you are a 7, taking the path of least resistance often seems to be the easiest way to deal with the dilemmas in your life. Take a hard look around you. Carefully decide which situations need improvement or change and which situations would naturally improve if you develop a more positive, forgiving, flexible or open-minded perspective.

For example, you might have taken on a new job, an exercise program or joined an organization. Let's say you joined a tennis team. At first the games were pretty easy and stress free, and you had a lot of fun. Then, after a while it seemed your teammates had improved and you were still playing at the same level. The competition increased and others started to tell you how to improve your game. Now you've become frustrated and you aren't experiencing the fun you had when you joined.

At this point, to deal with your feelings of frustration, you could: **1)** try to enjoy the game and not let other people's remarks stop you from having fun; **2)** quit the team and play the game with others; **3)** take up the challenge to improve; take lessons to get better and welcome teammates' comments for improvement. The action you ultimately take depends on what you feel is the most honest, right path for you and meets your needs.

At some point, unresolved issues evolve into potential crazy making and threatening circumstances. These issues can involve love relationships, family, finances, jobs, physical activities, weight problems and more. How often have you heard, "I thought I could change him after we got married," or "I knew we were using credit cards a lot, but I didn't realize we had gone this far."

Face whatever is unsettling to you. Confront it now. If everything is still genuinely right with you, you will know it because persistent thoughts of how you would like things to be will not be plaguing you. Keep your eyes open and acknowledge what you see. It's far better to look directly at the signs telling you where to make turns in the road and actually take the effort to alter your path, however uncomfortable it may be for a time, than to ignore the signs and face the reality years later that you're carrying an albatross around your neck. Although you can make changes later, it truly does get more difficult as the years go by.

If you are having trouble spotting potential unhappiness and disappointments on your own, find a safe, trustworthy person who will act as a sounding board or who will help you understand your situation better.

Having information about your options can be empowering. If necessary, make use of factual information you could obtain from an attorney or financial counselor, for example.

Also, if you have questions you want answered, don't be afraid to call on your intuition or outside help, as needed. Keep asking. The truth may be within, and when you don't listen to your inner guides, it's easy to make mistakes.

If you choose to seek outside help, use the information as an auxiliary to your own decision-making skills. Outside help is especially important to consider when you know you have made poor decisions in the past or if you get stuck in some rut that happens over and over again.

6. LIFE IS NOT SO GOOD. Here is a picture of a 6. He is scurrying to make sure he has covered all his bases, always frantic that he may have missed something. He knows that something is wrong, but he's not sure what.

If you are a 6, you are probably telling yourself the difficult problems of your life are workable, but, in reality, they are not. You could be bending so far to make things work that you are breaking inside. You may want to face the difficulty on some days, then on others, you go into denial.

The games you can play with yourself as a 6 are truly amazing. Why? Because you still have enough energy to fake it—but you are not making wise decisions to fully solve your dilemmas. You may, in fact, not be in enough pain to make changes.

Many people get the notion that if they pretend they are not aware of what is going on, they are not responsible for the consequences. We often teach this crazy reasoning to our children, and they apply it to situations throughout their life.

Here's an example:

Mary's apartment roommates had major drug problems. She pretended this wasn't happening. When the police knocked on the door, Mary was "shocked" to learn that her roommates were suspects in a drug deal. She told the officers that she had no idea what was going on. When the police found various quantities of drugs hidden throughout the apartment, even under her own bed, Mary had a difficult time convincing the authorities she was not directly involved in drug dealing too.

Wearing blinders or not directly participating in a situation does not automatically protect you from the consequences. Be aware of the people around you and what activities they are involved in.

What To Do If You're At Level 6

First, locate what's wrong, then consider your options. You may have to enlist some help to uncover the problem, and it may take someone who is objective to show you your options.

Look at your behavior patterns. Be honest with yourself and others. Acknowledge what is going on in your life. Uncover the problem. Those close to you probably sense that something is amiss. Perhaps they have already asked you about your moods and behavior. What did you tell them? More importantly, what did you tell yourself?

Again, seek counsel from people and professionals you trust. Also, remember to tune into quiet, peaceful and patient thoughts. Don't jump at the first idea that presents itself. You may find that your safest haven is right where you are, at least for now.

If you need to face some strong realities about yourself and your needs, don't procrastinate. Procrastination keeps you from fully living in the present. Ultimately, you are putting off your own life. Don't fear the pain of change. Change is a natural part of life. Facing a cup of pain today can save you a bucketful of anguish tomorrow.

As a 6, listen to your gut feelings. If something is continually eating at you, consider your options before you become physically or mentally run down. If you are going to make changes, be positive and thorough in thinking through the direction you plan to take.

5. SOMETHING HAS TO GIVE. One positive note about being a 5 is that you still have some energy to do something about your situation. However, you might be inclined to do it out of anger and hurt. Being a number 5 on the scale can impel couples to seek marriage counseling. Each one may be blaming the other partner, yet both realize the marriage needs professional help.

As a 5, you are in an interesting dilemma. You may be experiencing intense pain, hurt, anger and disappointment; however, it may appear to you that others are all at fault. Even if this is the case, don't overlook what you may also be adding to the situation.

What To Do If You're At Level 5

Discovering you are at this level could very well be an important part of your growth process. Progress often begins when you detect a stress level or pattern you may not have acknowledged before that runs throughout your life, especially if you have experienced numerous hurts and losses somehow connected with it. Perhaps old pain is just showing up in new ways right now, just in time for you to recognize the silver lining or the lesson to be learned.

If you are seeking marriage counseling, stop and look closely at the issues, perhaps there are some changes you need to make in your behavior. If you are angry at your spouse, it's time to stop and view the issues from both sides. Perhaps your frustration may be justified in some way, but you may be so attached to your own perspective you can't see another point of view.

Honestly study yourself from as many different perspectives as you possibly can. Think carefully to see how you are contributing to the problem. What can you offer as part of the solution? You may be upset about a present situation, or you may be hurting from something your spouse did in the past or both. If you are having trouble sorting out the various aspects of your problem, or you are unable to locate its source, you would probably benefit from professional help.

Be careful not to let your pain provoke you to react in a manner you will regret. If you are angry and the anger continues to build, you may resort to aggressive or even violent behavior, which would take you even lower on the scale. This will not benefit you or others immediately or in the long run.

If you are having trouble releasing painful past experiences, let your anger or hurt motivate you to work through the healing process, and work your way up the scale rather than down. Don't use the experience as an excuse to take your wrath out on others. Also, during this time, be sure to give yourself credit for handling your life issues as well as you are right now. Transcending pain and hurt is difficult. It requires much time and a lot of patience.

4. LIFE IS DEPRESSING and ANXIETY PROVOKING. As a 4, you are losing your energy and maybe even hope. Perhaps you are turning your anger inward and beating yourself up, believing life never works out right for you. You may have deep anger or resentment toward someone who has greatly influenced you so that you no longer trust your own judgment or feel you have any influence over your own life. Or, you may be grieving over the realization that you made a serious error in a love relationship. As a 4, you are feeling down and can't seem to get very much accomplished. You are consistently depressed and can't seem to pick yourself up.

On the other hand, you may be running in different directions, trying to achieve many goals at the same time and losing steam. However, you have no tenacity. You are unable to finish anything. In its own way, futile activity with no direction can be a sign of losing ground.

(For a number of people there is some biochemical activity in their brain which can predispose them to feel this way. This condition can exacerbate negative response to stressful or sad events. It can contribute to problems if it remains unchecked.)

At this point on the scale, if not sooner, you might want to find a mental health, psychiatric, medical, and/or neurologically-trained professional who can test you to see if your physical biochemistry is contributing to your life's dilemmas. For example, more and more adults are discovering they have been plagued much of their lives with Attention Deficit Disorder, oftentimes coupled with Hyperactivity.

This condition can prevent a person from achieving his or her goals in school, relationships or career. Angry outbursts, disorganization, and inability to focus are just a few of the symptoms a person can experience.

During the course of writing this book, I took a test and discovered I have Attention Deficit Disorder with Hyperactivity. Now, I am getting the medical, nutritional, organizational and emotional help I have always needed. Thank goodness I decided to continue my search for what it would take to raise my happiness quotient. Because I kept experiencing frustration and seemed to always be working so hard to get through certain situations, I took the test for A.D.D. Now, I am more aware of what I need to do to reach the high numbers and stay there longer even when events in my life have been quite stress provoking.

What To Do If You're At Level 4

It may frighten you to be at a 4, but it's also a good time to face reality before your problem gets worse. How can you spot your depression, anxiety or pain? Here are some signs:

✱ unable to sleep or wanting to sleep all the time

✱ unable to eat or eating everything in sight

✱ unable to concentrate well on a task

✱ vacillating on an issue

✱ feeling a sense of hopelessness about your situation

✱ feeling down, tense or irritable much of the time

If you are a 4, it is important to let others be there for you. This is no time to insist on going it alone. The healthy person gets help when she needs to. The person who is in real trouble often insists she has it together and doesn't need assistance from anyone. If you have not seen a counselor, this is the time to consider doing so.

It is also important to maintain your health. The more depressed you feel, the more vulnerable your are to sickness and the less attention you may be giving to your general well being. If you haven't had a medical check-up recently, and you don't feel very well, get one. Your body and your mind are intricately intertwined, and generally pain or sickness could indicate mental stress.

You may be strongly drawn to drugs or alcohol to relax now, or maybe you have done this before. However, you may actually be self-medicating and really need to see a doctor. If you feel you need something to stabilize your moods or your behavior, see a health practitioner. Taking substances on your own often prolongs and exacerbates your issues.

3. INCREASED CONFUSION. Every day seems like chaos. You are losing your ability to make effective decisions. You feel as though you are sinking into quicksand and you feel life will never get better. You may be disoriented to the point of not knowing which way is up or what problem you should tackle first.

What To Do If You're At Level 3

Remember that life moves in cycles and does not remain the same. Take a break from your surroundings if possible. You need a new perspective on matters. Changing your environment for a while may help, especially if you are taking a break from your regular routine.

Learn to sit still and take deep breaths. Find positive thoughts to rest on. Recognize the aspects of your life that are actually going well, and don't take them for granted.

Take walks and get your body in motion. Whatever you do, don't lie in bed doing nothing all day (unless it is a medical necessity or you just really need to relax to get your spirit and strength back). Read a motivational story or book or call a friend.

Meditation or prayer can be helpful. Sometimes a person does need to create some space for inspiration or to be sad, grieve or cry. Use this time well and decide upon a specific time to get back on your feet to get help and direction and to move ahead.

If you have been hit by a bomb, surround yourself with all the love and support you can find. Support organizations such as self-help groups can be helpful at this time or at a later date when you are ready to talk to others. Local mental health centers,

YWCAs, and the social services departments in hospitals often provide phone numbers for support groups and resources. Check your phone directory for Alcoholics Anonymous, Alanon and other supportive programs. Life was not meant to go through alone, especially when one is in great pain and anguish.

Think about other times when circumstances were difficult and remember how you got through those times. Write down the actions you took and rehearse them in your mind. Don't forget to give yourself credit when going through each layer of the problem. Also, recall how wonderful it was when in a nick of time, events turned in your favor. These are the moments when you realize life can be full of promise with a bigger picture and more possibilities than you realize. Let yourself know there will be a time when you will look back and remember that somehow you got through this situation all right.

2. LIFE IS A CRISIS. If you are down this far, you may be feeling disoriented to the point of needing immediate professional intervention. You may feel like giving up. Your mind could be saying, "What's the use. There's nothing I can do. All of the options lead nowhere." Stuck in raw fear (fear that can easily become panic), you are frozen. You probably feel abandoned, totally alone. You might even be thinking that you stand to lose everything dear to you, loved ones, friends and all financial stability.

As a level 2, you may be so confused that you are moving too quickly to think about the consequences of your actions. You are possibly in a powerful crazy-making mode.

What To Do If You're At Level 2

As difficult as it may be to face your issues, it's important to note that your decision-making skills may not be at their best right now. If you are inclined to be paranoid or if you tend to obsess about situations, try to realize this type of thinking blows everything out of proportion. If you tend to overreact and blow up, these emotions can work against you. Take one step at a time and cross bridges when they come to you. Don't take on more than seems necessary right now.

Seek help from those who are in a position to help you. As with someone at the 3 level, you may need to get help in areas you have probably never considered before—a supportive program, a grief group, a church or organization, a therapist or a psychiatrist. Choose a respected program or a professional whom you can trust.

Finally, try to keep in mind that with crisis comes new opportunity you may have never considered before. Major changes are definitely needed and this is the time to make them, but attempt one at a time rather than everything at once, if possible.

1. LIFE IS AT THE BOTTOM LINE. This level could be called "No Man's Land." You might be wondering if life is even worth living. You are probably in great emotional pain, and you want it to stop. Or, you may be wondering if you are able to face the consequences of what you perceive is before you.

You may feel as though the pain will never end and even time will not be able to heal you. Know that many people have been in this place before. Perhaps you have even been here before. This level is what some people call "The Dark Night of the Soul." When you get through this darkness, you may ultimately come out feeling stronger, and you might find you have more insight about life and people than you ever had before.

What To Do If You're At Level 1

Life may not improve right away, and you may have to face some very difficult experiences and some hard truths. However, this is the time to gather strength and ask for support. Get all the facts and information you need to help you through. Take one thing at a time. Just getting through each day may be your main goal now.

If at all possible, alter your perspective from negative to positive. Tell yourself there is a workable solution. Just because you may not see the solution right this minute doesn't mean it isn't there.

If you are a 1, choose professional help, if you haven't already. Go to self-help programs or support groups several times a week, as appropriate. You may need time in a psychiatric rehabilitation hospital or program customized to meet your particular needs. Also, take time off from your job or environment. It is important to spend your time with people who are non-judgmental, uplifting and helpful rather than with those who may only add to your pain.

Remember, there is a way out or a way to get through your problem. It is less important to have answers than it is to be willing to look for the real questions. The questions could be "What is really going on with me now?" and "Where do I go from here?"

"What help do I need right now?" Take one step at a time. Don't expect to do it all at once. During this difficult time, you will find out what you are made of, and you may well have more strength and skills to make a better life than you ever imagined. You've gotten this far. Let faith in life's process carry you when you can't carry yourself. If at any time you feel you need outside help, get it. Also, if you or someone you are with is in physical danger, call 911 immediately.

Where Are You On The Cognitive Stress Management Rating Scale?

8-10 Congratulations. You are managing your life well and you feel empowered. Your happiness quotient is high.

6-7 Begin taking a closer look at your situation. Realistically consider your options before you fall any lower on the scale.

5 Seek outside guidance for insight into your problems. You may not be able to see the whole picture clearly.

4-1 Recognize you may be going through an overwhelming experience. You may require more professional help and support than you have been getting. Give your predicament top priority right now.

It may help to know that no matter where you are on the scale at any given time, there is hope if you:

1.   are willing to face your problems or dilemma right now;

2.   objectively view the problem with an open mind;

3.   recognize when it's time to plan to take action to make some changes and know when it's time to alter your perspective on the matter;

4.   and acknowledge what you have to do to make things better. (It's not necessary or even important to have all the answers at once.)

Go over the scale once a day to regulate your progress. Do this until you are through your difficult period. The CSM Scale is a useful tool to decide if you need to make changes in your life.

Once you are over the hump, it's helpful to take at least a weekly check to stay on top of your situation. You may want to continue rating yourself daily.

Knowing what your stress level is on the Cognitive Stress Management Scale, and honestly facing it, can help you become proactive about your situation. Although your numerical level can change throughout the day, overall it will average out to one number.

If you are hovering at a lower number on the scale, it's time to pull yourself together and improve your life. If you are at a higher number, use your positive energy to increase your well being.

The exercises in chapter 3 will help you begin to deal with your overwhelming feelings within a realistic structure. This structure can help lead you toward seeking the help you need and perhaps assist you in making some decisions right now.

Your various concerns and worries may focus on current issues which are bringing conflict into your life. You may also be thinking about past issues that are creeping back into your life and are interfering with the present.

Effective help will begin to unfold the more you are ready to make use of it. Remember the saying "The teacher will appear when the student is ready." That is how we are helped in our lives. Are you ready? Have you learned what you needed to learn from this situation? Are you in enough pain to make some real changes in your life? You deserve to live a happy life and to raise your happiness quotient as high as you want.

You deserve to work your way to more happiness now. In chapter 3 you can get some useful ideas to create a new beginning.

TAME THE CHATTERING MONKEYS IN YOUR LIFE

S tress and crazy-making situations are frustrating enough even when we are only dealing with external dilemmas and conflicts, such as a car breaking down, losing computer files or being late to an interview. We not only have to face stress created from the outside, but we also have to deal with the stress going on in our minds.

Here's where the chattering monkeys can bring even more everyday crazy making into your life. Your concern about an issue can start the chattering—those relentless thoughts that jump around in your mind. It can be compared to packs of wild and excited monkeys babbling to one another in a forest. One starts and the rest get involved too, until all you can hear are noisy monkeys. You have to learn to stop these babbling thoughts so they don't take over and drive you crazy. Problems become serious when the chattering monkeys start taking charge of your life.

Do you have a lot of chattering monkeys shouting at you right now? Do you know what they are saying?

Chattering Monkey Issues And Thoughts

Chattering monkeys can be broken into two different components—issues and thoughts. Issues could represent any situation in your life which presents you with a dilemma. Thoughts are those ideas, feelings, perspectives and opinions you may have about your issues. Your thoughts actually determine how major or minor an issue is for you. Your thoughts may also help or confuse the issues even more. Although the two are interrelated, let's first take a look at them individually.

Chattering Monkey Issues

Chattering monkey issues can be about almost anything. For example, you may be torn between...

❅ buying a new house or renting one.

❇ fighting in court for child support or giving up the idea, at least for now.

❇ filing for divorce or trying to make your marriage work just one more time.

❇ trying to pay off all your bills or filing for bankruptcy.

❇ having your relatives over for one more harrowing holiday season or going away somewhere you really want to go.

❇ going back to school or looking for a better job.

❇ juggling your time between work, children, adult relationships, your parents and yourself.

❇ putting your child in an expensive private school or fretting over whether or not he'll survive in public school.

❇ coping with the politics and stress of your job or proactively re-doing your resume and seeking new employment.

While each chattering monkey issue is diverse in its intensity and potential consequence, the commonality of the issues involves the possibility of conflict or stress no matter what you do.

Chattering Monkey Thoughts

Chattering monkeys thoughts are those ideas parading around and around your mind in circles like a merry-go-round that never stops. We all have these thoughts. In fact, the chattering monkey thoughts may bring crazy making into your life more quickly and intensely than actual circumstances.

Your chattering monkey thoughts fill your mind with various messages about the issues you are dealing with. They can involve self put-downs, a sense of immediate or pending doom, over-reacting to a situation or just feeling overwhelmed. You may have a full choir of chattering monkeys or just one who creates a relentless solo. The number of chattering monkeys you have depends upon your habitual response to situations and how active your imagination is.

The chattering monkey thoughts are not hallucinations. In other words, they are not messages or sounds you are hearing outside of yourself. If you are hearing outside sounds and voices, seek help from a well referred mental health professional, such as a psychiatrist, as soon as possible.

The Interaction Of Issues And Thoughts

Here's an example of how issues and thoughts work together differently in each individual:

Four different women have decided to leave their husbands and seek divorces. The common issue among the four women is "wanting a divorce." But here's how their chattering monkey thoughts will differ.

Woman A is worried about how her grown children and grandchildren will respond if she leaves her husband. "I've never discussed our differences with the children, so they're going to be shocked. What if they side with their father and I'm left out in the cold? How do I explain to our five-and twelve-year-old grandsons why I'm leaving Grandpa. It's going to kill my mother-in-law.

Maybe I should wait longer, even though I can't stand my life right now. But, if I wait, I am postponing my own happiness."

Woman B is worried that her husband will commit suicide if she leaves him. "He told me he'd kill himself if I ever left him. He's tried this before, so I know he's capable of trying it again. Am I responsible for his behavior? Could I live with myself if he did kill himself? Would I be to blame?"

Woman C is worried that she won't survive financially if she leaves her husband. "We fight all the time and I'm miserable. Life is hardly worth living when he's around. Two attempts at counseling didn't work either. But, he's taken care of me financially for 20 years. I didn't finish college so I'll never get a good paying job. I'll have to give up my secure life. I like my lifestyle, but I hate my life. Security or happiness, what a choice!"

Woman D has wanted to leave her husband for several months. In fact, she left him once but came back because she was afraid she wasn't keeping her head together without him. While he bored her to tears, he was also the only person who had always stood by her. Since she was going to be lonely anyway, maybe it was better to be married and lonely rather than single and lonely.

All four women are feeling unhappy about their marriages but their chattering monkeys are shouting different messages.

A Positive Note About Chattering Monkeys

Your chattering monkeys can serve as wake-up calls in getting you to take proactive steps to solve your dilemma. However, if you ignore them and don't take action, you may continually vacillate on an issue. Many times you may become obsessed by a difficult situation and no matter which way you turn, the issue is overwhelming and often becomes seemingly unworkable.

Consider this for a moment: Life is full of seemingly unworkable situations. Maybe you feel you are in one right now. Possibly you feel that there is only one answer to your problem. However, take a minute and think back over other no-win situations that have occurred in your life. Maybe it seemed miraculous that you got through. Usually our rock-and-hard place dilemmas are more about our expectations and fear of change than anything else. However, at the time, it may not have seemed that way.

You will come to know the difference between constructive and or inspirational thoughts and chattering monkeys that just wear you down. For instance, inspirational thoughts could be: "Keep going, the light is just around the corner." Or, "Take one step at a time, and be calm." Your chattering monkeys are helpful if they propel you forward, not put you or keep you in more no-win situations. If your thoughts are becoming more obnoxious than the actual problems in your life, this may be an indication that outside help is necessary.

The following problem-solving and thought-disciplining exercise will help you deal with issues and thoughts (chattering monkeys) that are too often in your head. Keep in mind that you don't have to solve everything all at once. To hold the panic in check, take a deep breath, and then take a closer look at the different aspects of your dilemma. Options will unfold as you work your way through the exercise. The more open you are to accepting different answers (or to wait and ask more questions if the answers are not immediately apparent), the more chance you have of creating better options or realizing that they are already available. Life, in fact, is a balancing act between proactively moving ahead and sitting back and waiting. Developing an inner knowledge of what to do when is truly one of the secrets to living effectively.

Often, it is necessary to go through the exercise several times.

PROBLEM SOLVING EXERCISE

Bring your thoughts and issues to this exercise now. Go through the steps in your mind or write them down. Often, when you see your challenges in writing, they become more clear. They also may look less scary, like minor hurdles, rather than major obstacles.

1. CHOOSE AN ISSUE TO FOCUS ON. Consider all the thoughts bothering you now. Which provocations and/or feelings trouble you the most? Isolate the biggest one, the chief monkey. Although some feelings are interrelated, try to separate them and concentrate on one at a time.

2. CONSIDER YOUR OPTIONS. What are all the ways you can deal with your situation? Use your imagination for a positive outcome. Now is the time to take charge of any negative thoughts and not let them obstruct your thinking. Write down or visualize a minimum of three options, even if they seem like long shots. You don't have to like all your options

equally. The important point is to realize that you do have several possible choices.

3. **WHAT IS THE BEST THAT COULD HAPPEN?** What is the best possible outcome for your dilemma? If you have not been inclined to see the possibility of good coming out of this situation, take time to do so now. Try to visualize the good happening, and think how you will feel when it does.

4. **WHAT IS THE WORST THAT COULD HAPPEN?** What do you fear most regarding your dilemma? Realistically consider what the odds are that the worst will actually take place. Quite often, the odds of that really coming to pass are much less than you think they are. Even if the "worst" does happen, there will still be options and perhaps unexpected positive opportunities could result.

Don't give too much thought to the negative, however. Try to focus on the best outcome. The main purpose of this exercise is to increase your awareness of your strengths and positive avenues for getting through your problem.

5. **WOULD OUTSIDE INPUT HELP YOU?** Do you need another perspective or more facts to make a clear and effective decision? If so, is there someone or something—a person, a group, an organization or a book—you could consult to get a better grasp on the situation? Write down some options.

Your strength may be in reaching out for support and help. If appropriate, get references from others before using new support services. (Chapter 4 offers more information on where and how to seek outside help.) It is strength, not weakness, that allows you to ask for help and support. Many times when you turn outside for help, your inner answers become more apparent. In other words, outside help actually serves as a catalyst for inner resources to rise to the surface.

If possible, make use of one or more of these support systems before continuing to the next step. Be careful, however, consulting too many people may lead to further confusion.

6.   WHAT DO YOU PLAN TO DO? Considering everything you now know about your dilemma, what action do you plan to take? Allow for contingency plans in case something unexpected occurs.

You may be in a place in your life that calls for major change—doing things very differently from the way you've done them in the past.

Tap into your intuition before deciding if it's time to make a proactive decision and move forward or if it's best to sit back and wait, dealing with issues as they appear. If in doubt, it may be wise not to take immediate action. Meditation, prayer, or letting your mind go blank are effective methods. Answers often appear when you clear your mind and are open to new or unexpected possibilities.

7.   WHEN WILL YOU ACT IF AT ALL? Decide if you will:

a.   Act now.

b. Wait for a better time. Decide when that time will be.

c. Do nothing at all. Recognize that doing nothing is a decision. You move out of the "I am hopeless and helpless" victim role when you choose to say, "I am deciding to do nothing about this right now, at least for the time being," or "I'll step back and let whatever is happening take its course."

8. ENTERTAIN POSITIVE THOUGHTS. Whether or not you took action concerning your dilemma, calm your mind with positive self-statements to help you through a difficult period. Some examples are:

"I've handled rough situations before. I can get through this."
"I've gotten through life this far, I can keep going."
"I can deal with the consequences."
"Life is tough and so am I."
"I'm doing the best I can."
"This is one of my life's major challenges, and I will get to the bottom of it once and for all. Running away will only make it worse."
"Seemingly closed doors will lead me to opportunities I otherwise may have missed."

No matter what path we choose, we all take life one step at a time. It might as well be a step in the direction of hopefulness rather than hopelessness. If negative thoughts are swirling in your head, remind yourself that you can choose to focus on the negative or on the positive. You can even list what you want to think about. (It also helps to write down what makes you happy and what has gone "right" from time to time.)

9. **EMPOWER YOURSELF.** Whether you choose to wait for a period of time, or you immediately begin the process of proactively making decisions and changes, spend some time doing pleasurable mental and physical activities both indoors and out. If you want to engage in activities with others, choose the company of people who give you genuine support and make you feel good about yourself.

Write down the names and phone numbers of people who are genuinely supportive and will encourage you to take the best course of action at this time. Use them as adjuncts as needed, not as replacements for yourself. Do not continue to seek support from people who consistently let you down; you're only setting yourself up for disappointment, hurt and anger. Also, learn to find joy in your own company, even if it's only for a few moments at a time.

10. **DECIDE WHAT TO FOCUS ON NEXT.** If you've been successful so far in this exercise, move on with your life and concentrate on the present. Concentrate on what you need to be doing now. When a chattering monkey pops up again discipline yourself not to listen to the chatter all day and night. You can say to yourself, "I'm putting you on the back burner and I'll get back to you guys when I have the time to do something about you and not before!" You could come up with an actual time when you will do so.

When you learn to effectively balance your thoughts between the front and back burners of your mind, and focus on one issue at a time, you'll have learned a necessary and healthy coping skill. But it usually doesn't come easily and it requires practice and discipline.

If you start to ruminate again about your dilemma, go back through the exercise. If you need to work on other issues, go back through the exercise with each situation in mind, one at a time. This process takes time but it is worthwhile. The less confusion you have in your mind, the less confusion you have in your life.

MARTHA'S INCESSANT CHATTERING MONKEYS

At the beginning of the exercise, you were asked to find the head monkey—the problem troubling you the most, the one that's making the most noise in your head. This, of course, allows you to identify one issue at a time. But what do you do if all the monkeys are chattering at the same time and each one seems just as powerful as the other?

Here's an example of how someone can have too many monkeys screaming at one time:

Martha felt overwhelmed by all her problems. They seemed to have started when she and her husband got into a financial jam. They decided it was best to move in with her sister and brother-in-law to ease their monetary burdens. However, at the time they were only thinking about saving money. They didn't realize the living quarters would be cramped, and that she would not like living with her family again.(Even though

a lot had changed since they had lived together as children, she honestly hadn't faced the fact that she and her sister had many conflicts to resolve.)

Shortly after they moved in, the strain became too much for everyone. Martha and her husband began to have a lot of marital problems. It even seemed like her sister sided with Martha's husband, which made her feel like the whole family was against her. Also, to make matters worse, Martha was feeling that her own life was going nowhere. The monkeys shouted, "bad marriage, troublesome relatives and unfulfilled life." The clamor became so loud that Martha started to feel the only solution was to get away.

One evening, in the presence of her sister and brother-in-law, Martha told her husband she was leaving because she just couldn't take it anymore and could not stand to live with any of them. She turned and walked out the door with her suitcase in hand. She didn't even have a plan as to what she would do or where she would go. Then, to make the situation worse, when she got into her little pick-up truck and backed it out of the driveway, she accidentally backed into her sister's car. Martha was so upset, she forgot to look in the rearview mirror. She then had to go back into the house and tell everyone what happened!

She smashed into her sister's car at a critical time. She had humiliated herself in front of her relatives and husband and now she felt dependent on him in the midst of leaving him. And she hadn't even considered the legal aspects yet—she hadn't even seen a lawyer.

Martha was clearly unhappy. But without considering all the reasons for her unhappiness, she passed the buck and presumed her husband and her family were the root of all her problems.

Martha didn't take the time to sort through all her chattering monkeys and deal with all her issues one by one. As she began to examine her actions, she realized how often she had been jumping into situations without thinking ahead. She saw too, how she often became dependent on the very people she was trying to escape.

Eventually, Martha got through it all. After that horrible crisis, and realizing that she had nowhere to go, she ended up apologizing to her sister and brother-in-law and to her husband. It wasn't long before she and her husband got odd jobs, saved enough money, and went to live somewhere else.

As the situation for Martha and her husband improved, she examined her life more wisely. She went to a career counselor, brushed up on her job skills, rewrote her resume and found an excellent, well-paying job. Later, with the money she saved, she went back to school. Finally, putting all her ducks in a row, she still felt she wanted to leave her husband and she planned her separation by moving near her school and getting a part-time job.

Martha and her husband had been going to counseling apart and together, and he, too, worked on making his own life better. By the time they separated they had acquired totally different views about life and decided they would each be better off apart.

Years later, Martha became a successful, self-supporting business woman. Her ex-husband also started his own business after going to trade school. They both still had issues to work out on their own but both learned to face their own dilemmas and see their own part in a situation, rather than blame it on someone else.

Harness Your Chattering Monkeys

In addition to going through the chattering monkeys exercise, here are some other suggestions that will help you further control the clamor in your life.

❋ Stand back a moment and consider the idea that this dilemma might be inviting you to look internally at yourself and your own life even more than externally looking at others and their behavior. Be open to receiving insights that may not yet be apparent. Recognize that there may be a lesson to learn from your dilemma which you may not yet understand. Ask yourself what it might be. Tell your ego to step aside, and explore the possibility that your pride or notion of saving face may be playing a prominent role in the dilemma.

❋ Take time out from interacting with people who push your buttons. If a button-pushing friend or relative calls you and leaves a message on your machine, you don't have to call back immediately. You could leave a message on the answering machine at a time when she is not at home, saying you'll call back some other day. You may want to send a note with short message saying you've been too busy to keep in touch, but you will call later when you have time.

In reality, we all need a break from the intensity of complex and stressful relationships from time to time. That's not to say, however, that intimate relationship problems don't require an immediate response of some sort. They usually do. You might want to respond by saying, "Let's work through this problem, then we'll take time to sort out other issues later" or "I'll think about what you said, then I'll get back to you." These statements can help you stay calm while gaining time to gather your thoughts so you can make effective decisions.

Over time, you may decide to call back, have a deep discussion, write a letter, explain your position, or just let the relationship drift off. It depends on your closeness to the person and the intensity of your dilemma. Although it's good to have closure or full healing in relationships, it's not always possible right away, especially if there appears to be no mutual respect or meeting of the minds.

Sometimes everything clears up years later, and sometimes situations are best left unfinished until you are able to effectively express your feelings and not muddle the situation further. Looking at the "big picture" as well as examining how your buttons are being pushed, may lead you to realize you have internal issues to work out. The dilemma may be more about you than your relationship problems with the other person. So taking time-out from discussing the subject may be a good idea.

Also, sometimes you may feel that it would be best to let that person go from your life, other times you may decide to examine what the person is saying to see if you can gain anything by it. You can then decide to alter your perspective and remain in the relationship or situation, or alter your interaction, or just let it go. (If someone does offer you great insight, it doesn't mean that you are indebted to that person or must stay with him or her forever.)

❋ Try laughing at your chattering monkeys for a moment. Look for the irony in them. Tell yourself, "I look forward to the time when I can look back at this problem and laugh about how I got through it." Oscar Wilde once said, "Life is far too important to be taken seriously."

❋ Choose your mentors well. Make certain they have sound judgment. It also makes sense to seek help from people you feel comfortable around and can relate to honestly. If you are disappointed with the initial help or advice, get another opinion or consider altering your perspective. Take into account that the input you get from others may not be what you initially want to hear. When you are seeking help, prepare to receive new ideas and suggestions. You may gain a completely new perspective that is initially hard to face.

❋ Choose all your future friends and jobs carefully, for they are the vehicles through which you will learn more about yourself. Be alert for red flags—people or jobs which may represent negative distractions or lessons with high price tags.

❋ Take responsibility for the outcome of your dilemma. No matter what outside advice you get, the final decision regarding what you do about your life rests with you. You are ultimately responsible for the direction of your life no matter what sort of pressure or influence others may have on you.

❋ Don't expect immediate answers. Sometimes to get the right answers, you have to know the right questions to ask. Help and answers come from a willingness to be open minded and to listen for ideas you may not have thought of before.

❋ Call a close friend you can talk to or laugh or cry with.

❋ Clear your mind of all thoughts for a minimum of five minutes (longer, if possible); see if any answers come to you from within. You may get some clues to help you make a decision. Because thoughts so often get in the way, it may be helpful to keep your mind blank (or open) when possible, even when life is going well to be available to insights and inspiration coming to you.

❋ Pray if it brings you peace. Calling out in prayer can also be a way of calling in. The synergistic relationship between reaching outward and connecting inward is nothing short of miraculous. Somehow the very act of truly buying into the notion that there is some positive way through your dilemma can be very comforting even though the path is not yet clear.

❋ Decide who you can truly give you genuine support. There are always people who will get on the bandwagon with you, especially if they're dancing to the "misery loves company" tune. True support and friendship come from those people who care about you through the long haul and are truly happy for you even if their own lives are rocky.

❉ Recognize that you don't have the whole picture; none of us does. Parts to your dilemma (inner conflicts, outcome) are not evident to you now. Imagine yourself in a helicopter looking down at the entire drama—you view the beginning, the middle, the end. If you look carefully, you'll see the end. Tell yourself that your drama will have a happy ending. You have nothing to gain by picturing a negative outcome, unless it propels you to make necessary changes.

❉ Do something physical. Take a long walk, run around the block a few times or play tennis. Once you get started, you may enjoy it. In addition, taking interesting classes, or singing in a chorus will enliven you. Even singing in the shower is a great way for releasing pent-up feelings and energy. Commit to something physically exerting regularly.

❉ Harboring bad feelings from past experiences will keep you from fully working through your present dilemma. Think about past experiences and how you got through them. Weren't there other times where you wondered if you would ever make it? If you have gotten through rough times before, look at this as another challenge. Don't sabotage yourself by thinking, "This is the monkey that will finally get me." See it as a positive experience to lead you to live a happier life.

❉ Create positive, empowering alternatives for negative ones that pop up in your mind.

NEGATIVE	POSITIVE
"I can't believe I screwed up at work and made all those dumb mistakes. I'm going to get fired for sure."	"I'll go to my boss tomorrow and ask how to correct the mistakes I've made in my work."
"I am so overweight, I'll never get into my dress for my sister's wedding. They'll throw me out of the wedding party."	"I'll have to devise a plan to lose weight before the wedding and follow it through. In case I don't, I'll find someone to let the dress out for me."
"I'll never be able to trust my husband again after what he did to me. I'll have to leave him, although there's no way I can do it financially."	"I'll have to see if I can come to terms with staying with my husband after everything he's done. If I can't, I'll need to find an effective way to leave him. Either way, I realize I need to find peace and come to terms with my own issues."
"I don't know if I'll ever get through college. It's too hard and too much work."	"I can only do what I can do. I'll take fewer classes and more time to get through and get tutors if I need them. If necessary, I'll also continue to re-evaluate.

Here are some examples of how to replace negative thoughts with positive ones:

Train yourself to stop worrying. Your worry may actually cause you to suffer even more than actually living through the particular dilemma. In fact, the worry may become so intense you may even wish something terrible would happen just so you could stop waiting for it to happen. The worry monkey can be sheer torture. It's time to realize that worrying is a useless and futile activity, in fact, a crippling and dangerous activity. Go through the chattering monkeys exercise again. If your worry and stress continue, you may want to seek professional help, if it hasn't occurred to you before. Give yourself a lot of credit for trying to control this problem. So many of us need help to train ourselves to let go of our worry habits.

One way to combat worry is to try this anti-worry exercise. First, take a one-minute vacation from worry by focusing on something other than what is bothering you. Time yourself. See if you can do this for five minutes, then one hour, two hours, up to a whole day. Examine what happens during this time off from worry. You will probably realize that the situation was not resolved by worrying about it and that things actually worked out OK when you stopped entertaining all those negative thoughts. (I can re-member my father saying, "It's funny how the things you worry about don't happen and the things you don't worry about go wrong." This type of thinking could lead you to constantly worry. I decided long ago that worry is an unnecessary interruption to the flow of life, and I have long since rejected it as a worthy companion.

Silence Can Be Golden

People often speak about the healing qualities of silence. Some conclude that people would have at least 50 percent fewer problems if they cut out 90 percent of their conversations. Also, thoughtless comments divulged to others often provide the fuel for unnecessary paranoia. Silence will be more difficult for some than for others. If you are impelled to speak, ask yourself the following questions before relaying information to other people:

❋ Is it necessary for you to convey this information? Should someone else relay this or need it be conveyed at all?

❋ What is your true motivation for passing this on?

❋ Will this information really help you or others in some way, or are you acting as the messenger for your peer group by spreading juicy news? Will your words help to raise the consciousness of everyone involved, or will they invite all parties to sink to the lowest common denominator?

❋ In case you are the initiator of this data, is it possible you are setting yourself up to be hurt or misunderstood by confiding in people who do not have your best interests in mind? Are these people "safe," or are you creating another chattering monkey or potentially crazy-making situation which could blow up in your face or cause embarrassment?

❋ Which action will bring you more peace of mind in the long run—saying nothing or relaying this news? Is it possible you will get some satisfaction from seeing the response on everyone's face? One you may later regret?

❋ Is it possible that you are in a self-sabotaging mode which will create chaos for you and others?

If silence feels uncomfortable, take a deep breath and consider that the discomfort you feel now is nothing compared to the discomfort you might feel later if you share every gory detail of a hurtful secret about someone else with another.

If you feel the tension of silence is uncomfortable to others who may seem to expect you to be talkative, explain that you are trying to talk less. You may even surprise and amaze people that you can remain quiet. Eventually they may say, "I really like you because I never feel the need to talk in your presence."

Your silence may even help to calm and quiet others. Keep in mind it's not your job to entertain others (unless, of course, you are getting paid to do so).

Controlling the outside chatter and harnessing the inside chatter are great goals to attain and will help you achieve a more fulfilling life. (This idea has been prevalent in Eastern philosophy and is now more widely accepted in the West.)

Chattering Monkeys At A Glance

Mark the following page of the condensed version of the chattering monkeys exercise so you can refer to it whenever you need to.

Note: If at any time you are under moderate to extreme stress, and it's too much for you to handle, get outside help. Call 911 if you are in physical jeopardy.

QUICK CHECK CHATTERING MONKEYS EXERCISE

a. Consider your issues. Which is the biggest one?

b. What ways can you deal with it? (Think of at least three.)

c. What is the best that could happen?

d. What is the worst that could happen?

e. Is there someone or a service you could consult?

f. What is your overall plan to resolve this situation considering allowance for contingencies and feedback from others?

g. Will you act now or later, or will you do nothing?

h. Calm your mind with positive self-statements, such as, "I can deal calmly and effectively with the consequences of this decision."

i. Find people and organizations who are supportive. Make a list of names and phone numbers of people you can call.

Decide on a new focus beyond the chattering monkey situation and do it now.

Go over these steps as often as necessary. As much as possible, silence your mind. Clear your thoughts after each round, especially if they are getting in the way.

4

TO SEEK OR
NOT TO SEEK
PROFESSIONAL
HELP...
THAT IS THE
QUESTION

At some point while you were reading earlier chapters, you may have come to the conclusion that you would like to get professional help to deal with your current problem or to improve your overall mental health.

Returning To The Same Professional For Help

If you have received mental health therapy or counseling before, you may or may not consider going back to the same person. If you found answers to your situation, it will probably be easier for you to seek help again. However, if you had a very negative experience or you felt you were not helped, you may avoid calling another mental health professional. But don't give up because of your past experiences; you may really need professional help to get better!

As with other relationships, you may have to talk to a few different people to find someone you feel comfortable with. Know there is effective help available even if you haven't yet found it. Just be aware that it may not always come in the form you had expected. At any rate, it is important to get help in an atmosphere where you feel a sense of respect and you can reach your own conclusions without feeling manipulated or demeaned.

(Also, you may find other types of services to be more helpful than the more traditional programs you've already tried. Some people make use of a variety of services at the same time. See the back of the book for additional resources and possibilities which may suit your individual interests and affinities.)

Note: These services are not necessarily recommendations for you in particular. They are examples of some of the kinds of services that are available. It's up to you to decide what best suits your own individual needs and interests. Also, regarding previous negative experiences with professionals, perhaps you may want to consider that a factor contributing to the unpleasantness was you were faced with issues you weren't ready to face. Perhaps, you are now ready to confront your problems using the same professional as before.

What To Consider In Seeking And Receiving Professional Help

Every professional will conduct therapy or counseling in his or her own unique way.

While you may be able to research your therapist's formal training, experience, perspectives and approaches, it is not always easy to learn about his therapy methods until you experience one or more sessions for yourself. Your therapist's orientation in working with you results from his own life experiences, specialties, training and unique personality. No matter what form of training or background your therapist has received, however, he should provide you with a feeling of respect and absolute safety both emotionally and physically.

Counseling Versus Psychotherapy

Since "counseling" and "psychotherapy" mean different things to different people, here are simplified explanations to clarify these terms. PSYCHOTHERAPY generally involves clinical depth and more than a few psychotherapy sessions involving issues going back into childhood to get to the root of present problems. COUNSELING often focuses on a single issue or a few situations in a person's life. These issues range from marriage or divorce to weight problems. Counseling is also available for sexual difficulty and more.

No matter what the issue, it is often a good idea to examine situations in your past to discover if they still have a negative hold on you. Good therapy and counseling, when needed, makes use of your past to help deal with the present. It's not to be used to drag you through old hurts and keep you in misery.

Going Over Your Medical History

To get the most conclusive help, divulge your medical and mental health history, including medications you have taken for, with your therapist, counselor and/or psychiatrist. Physical ailments and medications can have a great impact on your mental health and emotions. Body and mind work together. It's most important to address your physical as well as your emotional needs.

Psychotropic Medications

While medical doctors who are not psychiatrists may prescribe psychotropic medications, such as anti-depressants, which deal with the biochemical needs of the brain, psychiatrists specialize in working with these medications. The thought of using these medications may frighten many people; however, most psycho-tropic medications are much safer today and have fewer side effects than the ones used a few years back.

"Whether used alone or in conjunction with other therapies, psychotropic drugs can significantly reduct the severity and dura-tion of mental disorders." (*Pocket Handbook of Clinical Psychiatry,* by Harold I. Kaplan, M.D. and Benjamin J. Sadock, M.D.)

If you are wondering whether or not a medication would be useful to you, consult a psychiatrist and discuss its positive and potential negative effects. Don't rule out using a drug because of past horror stories connected with a few of these medications. Psychotropic medications, when properly prescribed to suit your diagnosed problems and physical make up, can do positive, stress reducing things for you.

Medications may or may not be for you. If you decide to take one or more however, it's important to tell your doctor about other medications you may be taking so she can determine if one of them will interfere with another. Also, discuss the strength of the dosage. Maybe you need a stronger or weaker dosage. It may take a while for both of you to find the right combination of drugs or the proper dosage.

Assessing Your Therapist And Therapy Sessions

Consider these points before and during the time you are receiving professional treatment:

✾ Is the therapist's voice consistantly soothing, caring and sincere? A telephone call or a voice recorded on an answering machine may trigger a response from you. Your intuition may serve as a guide in helping you to decide whether or not you have found the right therapist.

✾ Does your therapist "mirror" or reflect your statements and expressions in such a way that you don't feel judged or belittled? You don't want to be treated as if you are a child and your therapist is the all-knowing parent or sage.

✾ Do you generally feel comfortable with the therapist, or do you try too hard to convey your thoughts so she understands? Do you find yourself beating around the bush and discussing less important issues? A good psychotherapist will provide you with a physically and emotionally safe environment in which you can completely be yourself without fear of judgment or not being taken seriously.

✤ Do you feel better about yourself when you leave your sessions, or do you feel worse? You have more than enough stress right now, so you won't benefit from criticism or put-downs from your therapist.

✤ Don't confuse criticism, however, with being therapeutically "confronted" by your therapist. During the sessions you may be upset by experiencing negative feelings you might have suppressed because they were too painful to think about. When this happens, you may face some truths about yourself that may be quite sobering at first, but truly helpful in the long run. These confrontations and connections made between your past and present are most beneficial when you know and believe that the therapist cares about you; that she is on your team and is truly concerned about your emotional growth.

✤ Does your therapist have experience and training in treating your type of problem? If you have particular issues, such as adoption, infertility, abortion, AIDS, physical disability, or sexual orientation issues, try to know in advance, if you can, the therapist's opinions about these issues, how well informed she is, and if this person can be empathetic to you.

✤ Is your counselor able to view your needs from YOUR perspective? Can he meet you right where you are? Or, do you sense he may be trying to mold you into a preconceived idea of who he thinks you should be? If so, you may want to seek another counselor. "Everyone has a right to his own self-determination" is an axiom known to therapists and counselors.

✤ Do you look forward to seeing your therapist, or do you go to the sessions because you feel obligated? Your therapist's job is to meet your needs. It is not your job to meet his expectations. After all is said and done, is this person helping you deal effectively with your life and to move on, or do you continue to feel stuck, anxious and overwhelmed?

5

FREE YOURSELF FROM CRAZY-MAKING DOUBLE BINDS

Break The Cycle Of Feeling Damned If You Do And Damned If You Don't

Sometimes you feel as though you are up against a wall. Maybe that's how you're feeling now. No matter how you view things, there appears to be no clear way out of your dilemma.

Perhaps you feel this way because of major conflicts with people, or maybe it's another kind of situation you're in that's made

—77—

you feel hopeless. In either case, you could be caught in a double bind with what appears to be no way out. Read on, because there is a way out.

What Is A Double Bind?

According to Webster, a double bind is "a psychological dilemma in which an ordinarily independent person receives conflicting interpersonal communications from a single source or faces disparagement no matter what his response to a situation." In other words, you receive contradictory demands or expectations so that any action you take seems to be wrong. You feel like you're up against a wall. (A double bind feels like a no-win situation.)

Double-bind situations creep up when you are most vulnerable. They are subtle and insidious; they quickly wrap you in a web of confusion. Often, you do not realize this potentially crazy-making situation until you are deeply involved, and then it appears too late to escape. Even if you want to let go of the predicament, you can't. You feel you have to fix it; it's your duty to fix it.

Without realizing it, a person can get into a type of "magical thinking" regarding double binds. It can actually seem easier to try to improve a hopeless situation, thus swimming upstream, so to speak, rather than face the fact that you probably need to alter your entire perspective on the matter.

THE CASE OF "I CAN MAKE IT RIGHT"

Jay's best friend from college called to say he was in town on a business trip and wanted to come over to see Jay and his family. Jay was excited and told his wife, Rhonda, how much he had missed Sam throughout the years and how he had never really found another friend with whom he could relate to so well.

In fact, he recounted the time when he and Sam had thought about going into business together. Halfway through his explanation he stopped, realizing his wife was not really listening. Throughout their marriage, Rhonda's response to Jay was less than satisfying; he felt that she never really gave him the attention he deserved.

Reluctantly, after some discussion, Rhonda agreed to have Sam over for dinner. That night Sam remarked how lovely the house was and how well life seemed to be treating Jay and Rhonda. Immediately, Rhonda remarked that they were doing well because of her father's money. Then she went into a full recital about how she had saved Jay from getting into a faulty business deal when they were first married by talking her father into taking Jay into his own business

Sam didn't say a word, but he noticed Jay slump down into the chair. Jay was quiet for the rest of the evening, and somehow Sam talked his way through the awkward silence. Rhonda, on the other hand, seemed quite content to putter around in the kitchen, feeling pleased with herself that she had put Jay in his place.

The following day, Jay did an unusual thing. He didn't show up for work at his father-in-law's office. Instead, he took the day off and met

Sam for lunch. He found himself talking about things he had never told anyone, but had been thinking about for years. He explained to Sam that Rhonda had in many ways let him know he wasn't good enough for her and would never make anything out of himself.

"I really didn't want to hang on for so long, but I wanted to stay in the marriage because of the children. I just keep thinking if I did everything Rhonda's way, she would somehow come to appreciate me, but she hasn't."

What Jay hadn't realized was that there was no way to please Rhonda. She had her own reasons for not being happy, and the primary one was that she lacked and wanted attention and affection from her own father. This had nothing to do with Jay.

Sam listened, taking note of how old and haggard Jay looked for someone in his early forties. He couldn't help but think that Jay had lost track of who he was in hopes of pleasing someone he, and probably no one, could ever please.

When they parted company, Sam said, "Look buddy, whatever you do, at least do something in your life that makes you happy, because nothing you do to please her will ever work."

Jay went home wondering if he should get involved with another woman or if should change jobs. But then he thought these types of changes in his life would not really solve his own issues. Jay was in a no-win situation. Part of that situation was the futility of making his marriage work, trying to please someone else when he did not really know how to please himself. He didn't know who he was or what he really wanted out of life.

Jay realized he was having a mid-life crisis, but he didn't know how deep or how serious it was. It almost seemed like it would be easier to fake his way through the marriage by trying to please Rhonda rather than facing his own lifetime plans and goals. In some way, Jay even thought he deserved Rhonda's treatment because he let her talk him into working for her father in the first place.

Jay was still young enough to change his life, but how? Were things really as bad as he thought they were? If he hadn't seen Sam, would all this have bothered him so much? Jay was truly in a double bind, but he didn't understand the complexities of it. He also didn't really see how far he was willing to compromise himself to try to "fix" his marriage.

Perhaps you can relate to Jay in some way. Perhaps you relate to Rhonda. She too, was in a double bind of sorts. She wasn't happy either, but neither she nor Jay realized they had other options. You always have more options than you think. It's really a matter of:

❋ how much you are willing to face

❋ how genuinely happy you feel you really deserve to be

❋ and how willing you are to invest your energies into another option.

How Do You Know You're In A Double Bind?

Three mental conditions take place simultaneously when you are caught in a double bind:

1. You feel trapped by a conflict or problem.

2. You are convinced you cannot escape the conflict or win the battle.

3. You feel compelled or have a strong sense of responsibility to do *something* to solve the problem.

Numbers 2 and 3 are the crazy makers, because you are driving yourself nuts trying to fix an unfixable problem. Emotionally brutal double binds can creep furtively into your life and into your relationships. Often, you don't see them forming, and you're not prepared. This is especially true if you are used to taking the blame for them.

Here are some questions to ask yourself to see if you are in a double bind now. They are also good questions to ask yourself at the start of new relationships. They may lead you to alter the course of your involvement, take another route or back out if necessary.

* Are you going round and round on the same issues with someone?

* Are you in the trap of not knowing what to do about the problem, but, at the same time, you feel that you *must* do something or you'll feel guilty? Or, do you feel it's probably your fault anyway?

* Are others telling you what you should be doing while you feel frozen, unable to move?

* Do you think that if you seek your own happiness or look out for yourself, you are selfish? Or, do you believe that if you take care of yourself, you will lose someone or something?

❊ Are you throwing up your hands and saying, "This is my lot in life. There's nothing I can do about it."

❊ Do you feel someone else or something else could save the day, even though no apparent solution appears to work?

❊ Do you feel that others who are involved in the situation desire a solution, or are they looking for a person to blame? If they do want someone to blame, could that person be you?

The more you answered yes to these questions, the more firmly you are stuck in a double bind. Practice will help you work out your own double-bind situations. Here are a few double-bind dilemmas to look at. How would you respond? What steps would you take to get yourself out of the quicksand?

Feeling Stuck In Everyday Interactions

Picture yourself in an uncomfortable situation with a person you are deeply attached to on some level. This person could be a friend, or a lover or a business associate. The relationship began well but is beginning to sour.

At first you cared for this person, but lately you feel put down and annoyed. There's too much tension; you feel frustrated. Somewhere along the line, the relationship became unbalanced. You feel like you gave your power away, but when you think about it, there was actually an imbalance of power from the start.

Up until now, you didn't want to jeopardize the relationship, so you never considered evaluating your interaction with this person. You felt you had too much invested to rock the boat or make drastic changes, because the risk would be too great.

Now, if the relationship is with your boss or a co-worker, the complications could affect your livelihood. And the old saying, "Think twice about rocking the boat if it isn't yours to rock," is running through your mind.

You may feel as though you are not being respected in this relationship. More and more you feel like you never say the right thing or come up with the right answer. Inside you are angry, and you take your anger out on other people. You may not even be fully aware of all this.

Finally, you come to the conclusion that you have to let this person know how you feel. Yet, when the time comes, you say nothing. The chattering monkeys start with "I'll distance myself...I'll be less available to him...maybe I'll switch departments." The tension is mounting. On the one hand, you are increasingly up-tight about the situation, but you can't bring yourself to confront this growing problem. Your stomach churns when you picture how this person is going to react to your comments and concerns.

You are in a double bind. The crazy making has begun. By now you are mumbling to yourself, "This dilemma is driving me crazy. I feel helpless. I don't know what to do, but I feel I should have control over it."

Political Double Binds In The Workplace

At the workplace, the stakes can be tough. Due to politics, salary levels and periodic evaluations, it's not always wise to express your true emotions. In this environment, you may think you will go out of your mind if you go to work one more day. The political smog is so thick you can scarcely breathe.

Assume you've spoken up at a meeting, thinking everyone was behind you. Acting as the group spokesperson (and self-proclaimed hero, although that may not have crossed your mind), you assumed your associates would all back you.

However, when the time came for the others to defend your position, no one said a word! After the meeting, your supervisor called you into her office. You were told you were not being a good team player, and that was too risky considering the possibility of future layoffs.

You're shocked. "Really, all I was trying to do was improve communication by giving honest input," you say. Of course, the boss doesn't see it that way. Besides, if she has been taking a lot of heat lately, transferring some pressure onto you may be appealing.

To be safe in the workplace environment, think before you give your true opinion, even when someone asks for it. Does the other party really want to know what you think, or does she really just want your support and loyalty?

Common Responses To The Double Bind

How could you effectively respond to a double bind? Depending on your past experiences and ways for dealing with life thus far, the following examples demonstrate how some people react to double binds. They include: *the occasional double bind; hanging around for the carrot; there-must-be-a-way-to-fix-it syndrome; being the scapegoat;* and *remaining the martyr.* See if you relate to any of them.

The Occasional Double Bind

If the no-win entanglement with someone occurs occasionally, and it involves a particularly sensitive theme such as body weight or financial matters, you may just chalk it up to it merely being a touchy area in this person's life. Learning to accept people as they are is one of life's most difficult tasks. If other areas of your relationship are fine, and if you truly value this person, then a few verbal confrontations may not bother you. You may just accept these occasional volleys and know they will blow over.

Nevertheless, the time may come when you want to discuss your feelings with this individual to clear the air. You might even be thanked by the other person for bringing this to his attention.

In a double-bind situation, however, the annoying issue appears more often, and is not something that can just blow over. Also, the other person is not usually grateful for your remarks or comments.

Here's a commonplace double-bind scenario. It shows how no-win situations get started and how easily you or anyone can become involved. Decide for yourself if you could live with the following relationship.

Between A Rock And A Hard Place

Your girlfriend asks you how she looks in her new dress.

You are honest. "You look great... beautiful."

"You're just saying that," she replies, "because you think it's what I want you to say."

You had no intentions of patronizing her. "No, really, you do look good."

"What you really mean is, I look fat."

This time you remain silent.

"I knew it," she replies. "You hate this dress."

You had no idea that your truthful compliment could bring your friend to an identity crisis; but your girlfriend's next statement reveals just how worthless she really feels.

"You always make me feel rotten about myself," she says, frowning. "You're always putting me down."

Of course, you have neither put her down nor done anything but respond in a positive way to her loaded question.

Unfortunately, there was no right answer. You were caught in a double bind. Chances are no one could have handled the situation any better. Face it, any approach you take to a confrontation like this won't get you anywhere. You are not going to win.

But worse than losing or being stuck is feeling that you are guilty, at fault, or even inept because you could not make this woman feel good about herself (certainly the sexes can be switched here). If this is what happens to you again and again in a relationship, take a long serious look at what keeps you playing in this self-deprecating drama. Try being less available when this person is moody. When you are with this person compliment her less often. Or, you might say, "You know, I never seem to say the right thing. What would you like to hear?" However, there is no guarantee this will resolve anything with her type of personality.

Some people rarely receive compliments, so when you do give them one, they're surprised. They may feel they don't deserve compliments. Deep inside they may also realize they were not treated well in the past, and they may react negatively when you trigger this sad reality.

Hanging Around For The Carrot

Perhaps your no-win situation begins to escalate and you find more often you rarely say or do the right thing according to the other person. On some occasions you may say the right thing. You tell yourself that the positive areas of the relationship are flourishing, but generally you are much like the donkey that continues to reach for the carrot on the stick even though the carrot is just out of reach.

After all, you've had a few "wins" with this person and that keeps the relationship going because you are hoping for more victories. When the other person is pleased, you momentarily feel good because that person seems happy.

Also, in this type of relationship, when the other person becomes very discontented and complains on and on about someone, do you smile, listen and wait for her to finish, but all the while "walk on eggshells," knowing that at any moment you could join the ranks of others who have fallen from grace?

If double-bind dilemmas with a few "wins" thrown in become familiar and even acceptable to you, take a look at what this is telling you about yourself. These double-bind dilemmas are like an old shoe. The tattered shoe is really quite comfortable, until pebbles get into it. Then you can't decide if it is worth the effort to stop and dump the pebbles out, or continue to walk along and adjust to the annoyance. It's amazing how much pain you will tolerate, especially if you get a small reward now and then.

Are You Always Waiting Around For The Carrot?

It's not always easy to determine if you're the type waiting around for the good stuff which will never come. Here are a few questions you may want to ask yourself.

1. Think about all your major relationships (work, school, club, marriage, family, friends). Is there a relationship that started out well but is now impossible more than 40 percent of the time? Are you hanging on to it because you perceive you get some type of benefit?

2. Does this person do something that you believe you can't do for yourself?

3. Does the relationship go back and forth from the sublime to the awful?

4.   Do you accept that anguish and suffering will always be part of your relationship with this person or situation?

5.   Do you feel that this situation is your only option, so you have to put all your energy into it?

6.   Do you take the attitude that others have it a lot worse, so you're really lucky to be in your barely tolerable situation?

7.   Do you feel that you are putting more energy into the relationship than the other person, and do you feel that more often than not that it isn't enough? Or, does the other person feel he still isn't getting enough with all the energy you are putting into it?

If you answered yes to any of these questions, you may be hanging around for the carrot, a carrot with a higher price tag than you can afford.

There-Must-Be-A-Way-To-Fix-It Syndrome

If you are caught up in the fix-it syndrome, you probably think a lot about turning back the clock to get another chance to do things over again. You have a burning need for the right response. Unfortunately, there is no right answer in a double bind. It was doomed from the start. Double binds keep you, as well as everyone else in a state of chaos. They are self-designed mazes with no exit.

If you are plagued with "there must be a right way complex," you might think it's easier and less stressful to actually stay and struggle to fix the situation rather than to accept your losses. The fact is, you would rather remain a victim in order to stay connected to the drama. Even though disconnecting could create a better life for you, perhaps, the thought of being alone seems too frightening at this time.

Again, it is important to remember that you do have choices. You are in the driver's seat unless you choose to hand over the keys to someone else.

Are You A Fix-It Person?

Here are seven questions to ask yourself to determine if a situation cannot be fixed by staying in it:

1. Have you tried everything, but nothing has worked?

2. Have you offered the others involved in this double bind a workable plan that would be helpful to everyone, but no one is interested?

3. Do you find yourself saying, "This situation would be fine if only the other person would change?" Yet, you are well aware that the other party will not change.

4. Have you tried to see things from a different perspective so the situation could be worked out? However, even when you change your perspective, is there still no resolution?

5. Does everything seem to get worse the more you try?

6. Have you learned anything or gained any new insight from this dilemma?

7. Have you considered the idea of "fixing" this scenario by focusing on what to change about yourself, and you've made some minor and even major changes but to no avail?

If you have considered all seven questions and tried them all, you may want to consider stepping outside the picture and emotionally pulling out your energy. This way you can run your own life without being entangled in the drama.

Those people who choose to stay in relationships and situations despite the fact they are barraged with double-bind messages would do well to consider the following points:

❀ Realize the other party won't change.

❀ Accept the person or situation as is without judgment; don't take personally negative statements aimed at you.

❀ Stop trying to make sense of the scenario; decide what makes you happy, and do it no matter what's going on. Recognize that the other party won't be happy with anything you do.

❀ If it's a work situation, simply do what's asked of you and go with the flow, all the while keeping your eyes open for another job. Work-related double binds are usually more about being a team player and agreeing with the boss than actually getting the work done effectively. Your supervisor cares more that you follow orders and show loyalty rather than save the day by pointing out the inadequacies of others.

If doing any of the above seems impossible for you to accept or do, you would probably do well to remove yourself completely from the person or situation.

Being The Scapegoat

In a double-bind situation, the person creating the double bind is always looking for a scapegoat, whether he is aware of it or not. For example, two brothers who head up a business may constantly fight. They may hire an innocent third party, such as an employee, for example, who answers to both of them. This person receives contradictory orders and may be blamed for things that go wrong.

The success of a double-bind operation like this depends on a sacrificial lamb. If the third party tries to side step the situation, he may succeed if he knows how to avoid being the scapegoat and remain out of the ring when the brothers start to fight. Otherwise, he may be drawn in when he is asked for his opinion. And, the owners may intentionally find fault with him.

Much has been written about the loser who gets the blame for everything that goes wrong in a family, which is where scapegoats are bred and nurtured. If you played this role in your family and didn't make an effort to stop it, or didn't realize what was going on, chances are you are still playing it with friends, co-workers, lovers, relatives, in-laws, professors, your own children and maybe even the man on the street.

There was Allen, for example, whose high-powered father needed a bone-marrow transplant. Allen was concerned about his own failing

health, so he refused to be tested to see if he qualified as a donor. This made his father mad. But, Jimmy, Allen's brother, willingly took the test and passed. He had surgery and provided the needed bone marrow for his father. Thus, he became the family hero. Allen felt rejected one more time and was further locked into the role of family scapegoat. Previously, Allen was in various circumstances where he was truly unable to help his parents, and they were very upset with him. Allen needed to realize, once again, that he was being asked to pay a high price for the love of his family, especially his father. He needed to see that he would be better off looking within himself and to others outside of his family for love and acceptance.

Are You Playing The Role Of A Scapegoat?

If you are uncertain whether or not you play the scapegoat role, ask yourself the following questions:

1. Have there been times when you could not tolerate a given situation any longer, so you pointed out the realities to family members or co-workers? Perhaps you were so blunt they felt justified in being insulted and angry with you. Maybe all you got was a blank look and rejection. They couldn't or wouldn't see your viewpoint. At some level, they may have known you were right, but instead of thanking you, they pushed you away. You became an outcast or were labeled a troublemaker. You became a little like the Greek messenger who brought bad news to the village and got his throat slit because the people didn't want to believe the news.

(You're probably not in a life-threatening situation like this, but you are mistreated.)

2.   Have you willingly become the spokesperson for a group of people who encouraged you to speak out for them as a group? Yet, when you did this, they all stood back and acted shocked. The expressions on their faces said, "This person is speaking for himself! We're not part of this."

3.   Have you been the brunt of jokes? People made fun of you while you sat back and thought, "I guess this is the way it's supposed to be for me?" You never questioned the role. Maybe you even liked the attention you received.

4.   As a child or adult, were you ever the scapegoat for someone's anger? They were really angry at someone else, but they took it out on you because you were available, or you felt you were required or willing to take it. Did they get away with it?

5.   As a child, if something was spilled, broken or missing, did you get the blame even if you didn't do it? If you made a mistake or didn't express yourself the way others thought you should, were you continually lectured about it to the point where you shut down?

6.   Have you ever been forced to take sides or referee family members when they were feuding? Then it ended and the family members kissed and made up. Were you then considered the instigator who started the fighting or were you just simply ignored?

Just one yes answer could mean you have been, and possibly still are, a scapegoat—a willing victim who stands in a negative spotlight. The more "yes" answers you gave, the more programmed you probably are to being a scapegoat. Take a closer look at the dynamics of scapegoating and try to determine how you play into the situation.

Remember, you do not have to be a sacrificial lamb for someone else's blind insecurities.

Remaining The Martyr

A martyr is just one step beyond the scapegoat. Not only does he get blamed for everything that goes wrong, but this person goes above and beyond the call of giving and gets nothing in return.

In other words, a martyr is someone who tries to fix a situation or to save the day by making a great physical, emotional, financial or legal sacrifice. Martyrs are also people who choose not to leave or to alter a situation to make life more agreeable. Many times the martyr acts out from a sense of guilt, worrying what others will say if he isn't overly generous. Or, the martyr will go overboard to be accepted, appreciated, even admired by others.

Perhaps the crazy-making of being a martyr serves a purpose for you. When people put you in a double bind, do you respond by throwing up your hands saying: "This is how it always goes!" "This is the price I have to pay to have people in my life." "I have no other choice." "I wish people would be good to me for once."

Let's look at the example of Allen and the bone-marrow transplant again. Had Allen gone ahead and further jeopardized his failing health by becoming a qualified bone-marrow donor for his father and undergone surgery, he would have fallen into the martyr category. Unfortunately, even if he did do this for dear old dad, he probably would still be regarded as the family scapegoat. And, if his health ended up failing even more after his sacrifice, his family probably wouldn't have given much support or empathy either.

It's possible to continue in this pattern of being the scapegoat no matter how often you are set up. You fall into a trap and you're not even aware of it. Unless you want to go through life as the victim, you are going to have to decide how long you intend to be a human dart board. You need to steer clear of this pattern and start taking care of yourself—building your self-esteem.

Are You Playing The Martyr Role?

Here are a few questions to ask yourself to determine whether or not you are playing the martyr:

1. Are you willing to give up your fondest dreams and goals in order to gain acceptance from others?

2. Do you tell yourself and others that you are tired of a given situation, yet you don't do anything to change it?

3. Are you too frightened to assert yourself, so you just go along with whatever everyone else wants? Do you go to extremes to avoid confrontation?

4. Even though you want to improve your circumstances, do you keep coming up with reasons why you must stay?

5. Do you stay in your double-bind situation because your uncomfortable safety zone seems better than taking risks?

6. Do you secretly feel that you are better than those who have put you in your no-win situation even though others in the situation don't seem to think so.?

7. Do you feel that even though they make certain demands of you, you are bending over backwards for those who persecute you so hopefully they will let up on you?

8. Do you feel it is your lot in life to suffer or to be the recipient of bad luck?

Someone once told me a definition of insanity. It is doing things the same way all the time and expecting different results. Are you in a pattern where the same things always go wrong, but you feel as if one of these times it will finally go right for you?

Stuck In The Web Of The Double Bind—Again

Here I go.
I'm sinking fast.
I feel I'm stuck in old times passed.
I cannot move.
I cannot stay.
That's how I feel throughout the day.

My feet are stuck in deep cement.
When I speak up, I just lament.
I know my words fall on deaf ears.

I'm so alone with all my fears.

I tell myself when I get out,
I'll learn from all this shame and doubt.
I'll try to do things differently,
but change does not come naturally.
I wish I just could get a break.
I don't know how much more I'll take.

I know a lesson's here for me;
I'm in so deep it's hard to see.
Is life this hard for other folk?
Am I the punchline for some joke?

What do I get from all this pain?
It makes me ill and warps my brain.
I'm trying hard to look ahead,
and side step from this spider's web
and help me pull out just in time.
Would happiness be such a crime?

I will not blame the other guy.
I'll view myself right in the eye.
There's something wrong.
I know that's true.
But "save the day,"
I just can't do.

I'll move beyond who's right, who's wrong.
I've got to sing another song.

I know that if I'm to break free,
I'll have to do things differently.

So for today, I'll start anew.
I won't get drawn into the stew.
I'll focus on my higher plan,
and help myself the best I can.
I'll try to tell my reeling mind
DON'T FRET!
IT'S JUST A DOUBLE BIND.

Barbara Ann Berg, September 30, 1996

How To Get Out Of Double-Bind Situations

Are you being asked to pay too high a price for love, affection and positive attention? When the price tag is too high in any situation, you lose dignity and self-esteem. Look over the following suggestions for getting out of your double bind.

Gradual Withdrawal From Being Set Up

When someone continually sets you up for a verbal battle over almost any subject, you have the right to physically and mentally withdraw from the conversation. You don't have to be an emotional punching bag. Initially, you may want to state that you're taking a five-minute time-out, then you will come back for discussion if the other person will behave in a more civilized manner.

You may also stop returning phone calls from this confused, so-called friend. Your job in life is not to be the recipient of someone else's frustration and inability to deal with his own life.

If your sense of self is healthy, you won't berate yourself for not being able to please this person who is really angry at himself or someone else. You will just know that this is more about him than you. You can walk away or at least take time out without feeling you are abandoning this individual. Continually being a sponge for someone else's emotional projections is certainly not the purpose of friendship or family.

If, however, you choose to continue the relationship, be prepared to set some boundaries, understanding that this person may never change, and may never get over his negative self-image which he probably doesn't even know he has. He may truly believe that friends or lovers should be willing to serve as scapegoats, victims who bear the brunt of his feelings of inadequacy. Discussing this matter with the person may not yield positive results. He will, most likely, focus only on your own inadequacies and not his.

You know you are successfully handling a double bind when you are conscious that there is no way you can fix the problem except to alter your part in it. You will also know you are on the right track when you realize that you often have to play a silent part as the "big person."

Taking One Step At A Time

Double binds take place in and around our lives almost every day. Once you recognize you have options, the more empowered you become to effectively handle the situation.

1. Recognize the makings of a double bind;

2. See one coming;

3. Get out of the way, if possible;

4. Come to terms with the fact that there is nothing you can do to fix situations for other people, unless they ask for help and truly want to change. Also understand that you may be able to help yourself;

5. Keep going as best you can;

6. Realize that you won't be able to please everyone and try to accept the fact that someone else most likely could not handle this situation any better than you;

7. Proceed with as little guilt, feelings of inadequacy or self-recrimination as possible;

8. Learn as much as you can from the situation so you can avoid future problems;

9. Recognize what draws you into double binds, maybe you're being everyone's "confidant";

10. Know that many double binds are inevitable and give yourself credit for recognizing when this is the case;

11. Take positive steps to keep yourself from the crazy making of double binds as much as possible.

No matter how often our eyes may be open, there are still times when we all find ourselves in a bad situation. The following affirmations may help you through.

Eleven Positive Self-Statements

These affirmations will help you improve your perspective and help you get through the roughest part of a double-bind situation. Perhaps not all of them may be appropriate for your double bind, but perhaps you can develop some positive self-statements, personal affirmations that will work for you.

1. There is a "right way" in situations like this. The right way is for me to think about my needs and to take care of them without leaning on others in this double-bind dilemma.

2. For my survival, I will cut my losses and stop banging my head against a brick wall. Accepting the loss will be much better than bearing the pain in the long run.

3. I'm not going to take this anymore! I deserve better and I'll make sure my own attitude or behavior isn't setting me up.

4. I refuse to take the blame any more for this problem. People will say and think what they may, but I'll keep going along my own path without becoming tangled up and having to defend myself.

5. Starting right now, I am going to stop trying to make an unworkable situation workable.

6. I'm getting off this treadmill and I'm going to start living now.

7. This dilemma is not my responsibility.

8. It is not up to me to fix everyone else's problems.

9. I am not going to act like a sitting duck.

10. No one else could do this any better than I.

11. I won't go overboard trying to explain my actions. Friends don't need to hear it and enemies won't believe me anyway.

Saving Yourself From The Workplace Double Bind

Always take note of the political climate before you voice you opinion at work. There will be times when you will be asked for your opinion, but be cautious. It's often best to keep a low profile, especially at first. This doesn't mean you're playing a coward. You're just playing it smart.

Even if you feel trapped in a situation, you may not have to respond right away. You could say you have to think about it and get back to those who asked for your opinion at a later time.

Talk to someone who could give you some ideas, maybe some insight and support.

Perhaps, if you sit tight for a while, the whole thing could soon blow over. This may also be a good time to look for another job. Always keep in mind that you have more options than you think.

Even though you may find it's difficult not to speak up right away, resist the temptation to do so. If you are cornered and asked for your opinion, and you feel you are being tested, you might say something like, "Gee, you'll have to fill me in with more information. Why don't you tell me what you think?" Now the ball is back in his court. You could also say, "You know, that gives me a lot to think about. I'll have to mull it over."

Don't feel like you have to play the hero. Mighty Mouse and Superman put together couldn't save the day. Neither can you, so don't try. Instead, step back and calmly assess the situation.

The following case history describes someone who broke through and altered her double-bind situation at work.

RENEE'S PATH IN BREAKING HER DOUBLE BIND

Renee was a woman who successfully learned how to get out of a self-made double-bind predicament. Renee's childhood abuse and trauma were of a severe mental/emotional nature. While she was growing up she received many mixed messages about life, and did not recognize the impact of these messages until she engaged in psychotherapy as an adult.

Renee had a childhood that was difficult by most people's standards. Yet, as with many of us, her feelings about her childhood were ambivalent. Sometimes, it seemed tolerable to her, other times it was impossible.

Renee was the oldest of four children. Her father was like a spoiled child, a needy alcoholic who saw people in the family as objects to meet his needs. He mainly expressed anger. He would beat Renee's mother, especially when he was drunk.

Renee felt that her mother cared for her as best as she could. However, Renee recalled that her mother was frequently ill, slept excessively and often left home for weeks at a time. She also took several medications for various reasons. By the time Renee was seven-years-old, she had learned ways to win her mother's heart and support when her mom was available.

Renee also recognized that her father didn't care who got the brunt of his anger. He directed physical blows and verbal tirades to any family member who happened to be nearby when he flew into a rage.

At the tender age of seven, Renee enrolled herself in the family drama as the dysfunctional scapegoat with the compulsive need to be the underdog and hero child. Her great purpose in life was to rescue her mother from her father's abuse. This, she believed, would help her mom retain enough energy to focus in a positive way on Renee. Although it was complicated, Renee sometimes was able to get her mother's attention.

Dysfunctional or crazy-making families affect their children in untold ways. The children learn to pick up crumbs of love and attention by whatever means possible. Unfortunately, they may continue in this pattern for the rest of their lives. Thus far, Renee had gone through life believing that in order to enjoy the pleasure of love and success, she must willingly take abuse from others, play the everlasting scapegoat, and be the one to blame for everything.

Even to this day, Renee finds herself saying, "It wasn't all that bad," when, in fact, it is truly amazing how much she went through and still retained her sanity.

Now at age 36, Renee found herself going into her second marriage while having grave difficulties at work and in her personal life. She was afraid of another marriage resulting in divorce.

After a couple of therapy sessions, it became evident that as a child, Renee had been involved in a number of complicated double binds. Still, she was initially unaware of how complex these situations were. When her growing understanding of the scapegoat phenomenon and her need to save the day as a wanna-be hero came to light in therapy, she began to make headway.

In sessions, Renee talked a great deal about the temporary department management job she was filling at the bank while the regular manager, Christine, was out on surgical leave. Renee was excited about the challenges of this new position. She was also zealous because in her old wanna-be scapegoat-hero style, she saw the job as an opportunity to prove herself. She was not aware however, of the dangers in trying too hard in a politically fragile work environment.

During the four months that she served as temporary manager, the teller morale went up, positive customer feedback skyrocketed, and no customer ever had to wait in line more than five minutes.

Renee was incredibly proud of herself. She was elated every time one of the employees stated how glad she was to have her at the helm. But somewhere in the excitement, everyone seemed to forget that Christine would be coming back. Well, not everyone had forgotten.

The vice president at the main bank, the man to whom she reported daily by phone, seemed only mildly pleased with her accomplishments. And, Renee sensed that the tone in his voice was not always as appreciative nor as positive as she had wanted it to be. In fact, the more significant changes our heroine made, the less enthusiastic he had become.

Then, shortly before Christine was scheduled to return to work, the vice president paid Renee a visit. Almost as soon as the man opened his mouth, Renee's stomach began to churn with anxiety and her heart sank with the foreboding old feelings of pending rejection. Just when she thought she had done all that had been requested of her, the vice president explained in his monotone that Renee had "shown up" Christine.

"We're not sure just where to place you when Christine comes back. We don't want the employees at your branch looking to you instead of Christine for answers. That would cause a rift among the staff," he said.

A few days later, Renee was made supervisor of the drive-through window. This position felt like a slap in the face to Renee. However, a staff member in Human Resources explained that the new position was a lateral move from her old position. She was told she should not have expected any long-term gains from her temporary assignment. Of course, it would be noted in her employee file that she had done a good job as temporary manager.

With no more than a curt smile from Christine and whispered promises of loyalty from other tellers, Renee took her new position at the drive-through window. As customers continued to ask for Renee, Christine complained about the unauthorized changes that had been made in her absence. Renee realized that she needed to get back into Christine's good graces, but she had no idea how. She felt utterly helpless and had no idea how to improve the situation. She was trapped in a double bind.

It was at this point that Renee decided to get therapy. Renee began to realize that the harder she tried to please Christine, the more she was mistreated. She began to understand her pattern of looking for positive reinforcement from people who were not inclined to appreciate her efforts. All through her life, she had made herself vulnerable to people who were not playing on her team. The vice president at the bank did not care about her excellent performance; her responsibility had been to fill in and keep a low profile, not shine like a star.

Eventually Renee found another job. And, she made a point of not looking to her supervisor for too many strokes. As time went on, Renee thrived at her new job. She no longer overcompensated to outdo others and prove herself, but instead she put out the energy required without over-or under-doing things. This pleased her supervisors. She had learned that the workplace, like life, has many crazy aspects and she did not have to fix them. Renee found life at work went smoother when she calmly went with the flow of events and organizational changes.

Recently Renee received a promotion. She now felt that her life didn't depend on her proving herself. All she needed to do was to be competent in her work and to not try to outshine everyone else.

Self-Observation

Take a few minutes to observe your own life—past and present. Don't look at yourself with criticism, judgment or scorn, simply observe how you deal with life. Are you living your life in a relentless search for approval from people who probably are not really supportive of you? Are you placing yourself in situations where you are likely to receive criticism and rejection? And as you stick your neck out and try to help others, do they often hurt you?

If so, be kind to yourself and know that you will learn your lessons when you are ready. Look around and see what you might do differently.

If you are doing well, at this point in time, chances are you have the ability to objectively look at your old pains. Possibly you have worked through them already. However, if you are still experiencing problems, you are probably repeating the double binds of your past.

Think about those no-win situations in the past as well as the present. As you read the second half of this book, think about all these double-bind situations in relation to the anger and hurt you feel now. As an adult are you finding yourself in no-win situations that seem to have an air of familiarity about them? Do they remind you of childhood problems? Or, maybe you are forming new patterns and insights. Whatever the case, read on and give yourself credit for getting as far along in life as you already have.

SECTION II

THE MOST DANGEROUS CRAZY MAKING OF ALL:

THE THINGS YOU TELL YOURSELF

Everyone has mind chatter. Unfortunately, the feelings you have inside can easily turn into negative, self-deprecating babble. Negative thoughts and conversations you entertain in your own mind can represent the most frightening and dangerous everyday crazy-making experiences. Because it's habitual, you often don't realize you are programming yourself into everyday craziness. You, as well as many other people, have developed a lot of negative self-talk from parents, relatives, and other well-meaning, or not so well-meaning people in your life.

Combine this negativity with your chattering monkey issues, and you can work your thinking into such a crescendo it's a wonder you manage as well as you do. Ultimately, you must learn to control your level of negative self-talk.

Chapters 6 through 9 are designed to help you get through those times when you are overwhelmed by your own inner feelings of not being good enough, or being angry, or feeling hurt or very disappointed about life in general. You'll also find resources and ideas that will help you bring out the best in yourself now and will also help you for the rest of your life.

All in all, you'll gain new perspectives to help you understand that issues and dilemmas are simply a part of life. You can learn to view them as positive challenges. Problems and hurdles will never go away altogether. Nevertheless, joy is something you can find in the midst of all your travails. In order for you to be happy, everything does not have to be perfect.

Before you move further into the next section of the book, however, let's go through an exercise that will help you tune into your own inner mind chatter. After the exercise, Section II also provides information about patterns and habits you may have developed in your communications with others.

REVEAL YOUR INNER MIND CHATTER EXERCISE

Judith Pillsbury, an extremely intuitive person and an excellent personal growth consultant, in Claremont, California, offers the following suggestion:

"When you want to deal with your inner mind chatter once and for all, get a watch that has an alarm. Set the alarm to beep on the hour. When it beeps, take a few moments off from what you are doing. Reflect on your self-talk during the previous 60 minutes. What were your thoughts about? What were you telling yourself? How did you feel?"

Do this exercise for a few hours a day over a period of several days or weeks, if you so desire. Consciously take note of conversations with yourself, and the thoughts coming into your mind. If you want, write them down so you don't forget. If your thoughts are usually negative, they may have become part of your consciousness like gobs of old chewing gum stuck on cement. Over time it gets harder to remove.

If you're like most people, your thoughts reflect many things—not getting enough done, apprehension about people or work situations, anger directed toward yourself or someone else about something said or done, concerns about not being adequate, or mulling over all the things that are wrong in your life.

If, after you've completed the exercise and you've analyzed your destructive, depressing or disturbing thoughts, take time to develop a few phrases that will keep your mind on a positive track to counteract them. For example, the next time your watch alarm beeps, you might want to say to yourself:

❀ I'm not going to let my problem get me down; not only can I handle it, but I can grow from it.

❀ How can this situation improve my self-awareness?

❀ Happiness is just around the corner, if I am open to it.

❀ How can I restate my negative thoughts so I can improve my attitude?

❀ I am filled with enthusiasm for all the good that life holds for me. Even painful situations are insights in disguise.

❀ I'm doing the best I can, and I am really impressed with how well I am doing.

❀ I will just do what I need to do and not get all shook up.

❋ I am dealing well with people today.

❋ Even in the midst of my problem, I look forward to seeing my best friend today.

❋ Here's an interesting dilemma. What can I learn from it?

Consciously fill your mind daily for one week with positive statements. Check in on the hour. You really have nothing to lose by trying this exercise. In time, you will more clearly recognize the negativity you have been entertaining and you'll have the ability to switch your negative mental activity to a positive frame of mind.

Communication Starts From Within

Although you may not fully realize it, you have a set of communication patterns you use in your verbal interaction with others. A number of these patterns have come about from feelings of hurt, anger, disappointment or rejection.

Common communication patterns, include *minimizing your feelings; acting non-assertively; delaying your response; being aggressive, or most effectively, being assertive.* Do you fit in any one of these patterns or are you a combination of bits and pieces of them all?

AN EXAMPLE OF MINIMIZING FEELINGS

If you are someone who minimizes your feelings, you may identify with this example.

Susan remembers an incident from high school many years ago when she

went out on a date with a fellow she had a crush on named Mike. Mike had just broken up with Marilyn, a popular girl from the "in crowd." Because Marilyn had trouble accepting Mike's breakup with her, she spread the word around that Susan had cold-heartedly stolen him away from her.

When Susan found herself ostracized by all her so-called friends, she came home crying to her mother. As usual, Susan's mother told her to stop all the fuss and not to make such a big deal over nothing. But to Susan, the incident was important, and this particular experience actually affected her more than other past incidents.

Susan regretted revealing her feelings to her mother. In fact, she felt more depressed because her hurt feelings were now minimized and discounted. Susan then decided, although probably not on a completely conscious level, to make a deadly pact with herself that she'd never be vulnerable in front of anyone again, including those closest to her.

Susan went back to school the next day acting as if nothing bothered her, although she was dying inside. After a while, everything eventually blew over, but she was never quite as close to her friends again. Susan had minimized her pain by acting as though nothing bothered her, when in fact it did.

Over time, Susan convinced herself she could handle anything. No one ever realized how much she hurt inside, not even Susan herself. Years later, Susan found herself in therapy. At the time, Susan was angry towards her fellow employees, and she admitted it to the therapist. She felt that others seemed to get away with taking more sick time off or making personal phone calls, but no slack was ever allowed her. In therapy, Susan came to realize that she didn't ask for special time off or get any privileges because deep down she was afraid her supervisor would minimize her needs just like her mother had done.

When Susan chose to shut down her feelings, she ended up with a chip on her shoulder that kept others from empathizing with her. She had set herself up to be misunderstood, alone and alienated. Other people had no idea how sensitive she really was.

Are you a "minimizer?" Do others cast off your feelings and minimize you? Is it possible you minimize your own dilemmas or those of others?

Consider these three points:

1. Do you feel others get understanding and empathy from you when they need it, but you always "have" to be strong for others?

2. If someone needs help, are you generally there? But, when it's your turn for help, they don't reciprocate?

3. Do you find when you let others know you are hurting inside, they don't know what to say or seem to say the wrong thing?

If you said yes to any or all of these questions, you may want to look at yourself in depth. Are you setting yourself up for alienation and misunderstanding because you minimize your pain by trying to seem more tough than you really are?

AN EXAMPLE OF NON-ASSERTIVENESS

Rick was the type of guy who would do anything for anybody, even if he couldn't stand doing it. While people saw him as a nice, easy-going, good-natured guy, he was actually always seething inside. It never occurred to him to say "no," although underneath he was annoyed that everybody walked on him, treating him like a doormat.

Rick was the perfect example of a non-assertive person. If he got crumbs from people, he rationalized to himself that he had good reason to stay in the situation. In reality, Rick was so frightened over the idea of confrontation and standing up for himself, he would justify doing almost anything to avoid possible problems.

Because he looked at life non-assertively, Rick never got what he really wanted. His non-assertiveness also kept him from voicing his opinion on the off chance someone might disagree with it.

Are you non-assertive? Ask yourself these questions:

1.   Do you ever ask anyone to go out of his way just a little so you can get your needs met? For example, would you be too intimidated to cut in line at the grocery store if you have one item and exact change, and everyone in front of you had a cart packed to the gills? Would you wait at the end of a line in an emergency room when you or your child is bleeding?

2.   Do you ever need to get something done or get somewhere

at a particular time, but you put it off or don't do it because you've been asked to cover for someone or do something for him and you don't want to feel his rejection if you say no?

3. Do you have good ideas to share with others, but you never say them? You simply listen to what they have to say as if you agree with every word knowing full well they are wrong?

If you answered yes to these questions, you may need help in assertiveness training. Assertiveness comes from taking risks and realizing your needs are just as important as anyone else's. Everyone is important and everyone counts. Perhaps you are not conducting your life as if this were the case.

AN EXAMPLE OF DELAYED RESPONSE

Ann spent the first 45 years of her life somewhere between being in shock and being numb. When someone treated her unfairly, she acted as though everything was fine. However, minutes, hours, or days later, she would explode as if a timed-release bomb went off inside her. And it had.

Ann's parents were skilled at making innuendoes or constructive criticisms over every little infraction, subtly implying that Ann wasn't good enough regarding this and that. Over time, it seemed that when Ann voiced her feelings or asserted herself, people either ignored or rejected her. She came to the conclusion that the only way she could be accepted was to act as if everything was just fine, even when it wasn't. However, her suppressed feelings would eventually surface. Inevitably she would explode and alienate everyone when the pressure got to be too much.

Over time, Ann learned that this "delayed response" technique back-fires and she came to understand her fear of confrontation. As she worked on being more assertive, Ann decided to speak up sooner rather than later, even though it felt terribly uncomfortable. She ultimately found that the pain of facing the music early wasn't as bad as carrying her anger around.

Do you use "delayed response" as an inner mechanism of communication which ends up as an outer explosion? Consider the following questions:

1. Do you like to perceive yourself as a mellow, happy-go-lucky person, when in reality you are often angry and mad at people who don't seem to respect or even to recognize that you have needs and boundaries too?

2. Do you feel you shouldn't have to explain to others about what bothers you? Do you feel they should already know?

3. Do you find you are afraid to say anything at all to a particular person because once you get started, you may end up telling him off and making things even worse than they were before?

If you answered any of these questions with a yes, you may be suffering from the "delayed-response" syndrome. If so, work on staying in touch with your feelings. Take small risks at first by letting others know how you feel as soon as it occurs to you that something is amiss.

AN EXAMPLE OF AGGRESSIVENESS

Roger moved through life like a bull in a china shop. He would quickly get out of control if he was crossed in any way.

Roger thought things worked out well most of the time, because people were so solicitous of him to his face. He was agreeable as long as everyone seemed to go along with his program when he was around; he didn't much care what went on when he wasn't around.

What didn't seem to go well for Roger, however, was his close relationships—people were always stand-offish or they weren't willing to become or stay involved with him. He never seemed to keep a girlfriend, and he didn't understand why.

Roger was always so sure he knew the right way to do everything, and, to him, people just didn't measure up. His aggressive and gruff behavior won the small battles, but he lost the war.

Roger, at age 40, had yet to learn that there are more effective ways to approach people as he went from job to job and from relationship to relationship. Underneath his tough exterior, he was so afraid of being seen as vulnerable, he scared people and held them at arm's length. People actually never knew how scared Roger was within himself.

Perhaps you can relate to Roger. In fact, you may not see yourself as aggressive. You're so busy making sure you don't get taken by others you end up alienating everyone in the process.

Consider the following questions regarding aggressiveness and how it relates to you or to other people you may know:

1. Do you feel you're a good person, but others are just out to get you?

2. When you are rough and aggressive with people, are you just protecting yourself?

3. Does it annoy you to the point of anger that others don't do things your way?

4. Are you afraid that if you are calm and easy going, people will take advantage of you? You'll be taken for a chump?

5. Do you feel you'll have no power unless you continually show everyone who's boss?

If you answered yes to any of these questions, you may have an aggressive streak that doesn't work in your favor. If so, think hard about how life has treated you. To obtain some insight into yourself, you may consider getting some help from a therapist or support group involving anger management.

Getting feedback from others may not be what you want to hear, but in the long run it will be helpful, especially if it is given in a kind, supportive way. Altering your communication pattern from aggressive to assertive isn't easy. When moving from being aggressive to assertive, it's important to get in touch with your feelings and let others know you are concerned about something before you are at a breaking point or are fed up.

Stress and anger management groups can be very helpful. You can also attend communication classes where you can role play. Become aware of you feelings along the way by checking where you are on the basic Cognitive Stress Management scale. If you are a 6 or a 7, speak up in a positive manner if you can. Don't wait until you are down to a 2 to take action.

AN EXAMPLE OF ASSERTIVENESS

John was really well liked by others. He had a way about him that invited people to feel good and comfortable. If he had a bone to pick with someone, or a misunderstanding to resolve, he generally approached the person with a sense of respect so they both could find a solution.

John was the kind of person who didn't jump to conclusions about people. He liked to give people the benefit of the doubt, but when he felt he had to confront someone, he did not hesitate. He instinctively knew it was easier to resolve a problem with someone sooner rather than later. So he usually brought up an issue when it first occurred, and before it got any worse. John's assertiveness also helped others to be assertive. If they needed to resolve a problem with him, they felt he was approachable. They knew he would listen and treat them with respect. John was a fair and honest person.

People with an assertive approach to life tend to feel good about themselves, others, the world and life in general. Usually, they treat others with respect, and in turn, they are treated with respect.

Perhaps you are assertive for the most part. Many people are. You can be direct with people who are easy to approach, but sometimes it's necessary to be assertive with people who aren't easy to talk to. Consider the following questions and points to determine for yourself how assertive you really are:

1. Are you aware of how you feel in almost any given moment without being overly analytical about it?

2. Can you pinpoint the time when something begins to bother you? Do you deal with it before it gets out of hand?

3. Do you make sure you meet your own needs without having to step on other people's toes; and, if you offend someone by mistake, can you apologize and get over the incident without beating yourself up about it?

4. Are you willing to deal with a situation or person even when you feel uncomfortable or disturbed about it or the person?

5. Are you willing to look at things differently if you think a change in your perspective would help?

6. Do you generally deal with dilemmas before they keep you from focusing on anything else?

If you answered yes to most of these questions, you most likely have a good sense of assertiveness.

Of course, like with anything else, it's easier for us to be assertive around those who don't seem to give us a hard time. For those individuals who appear to have no regard for the rights of others, keep in mind that when you assert yourself with them, it's more about your holding your own and hearing yourself speak up for your own sense of self-respect rather than actually trying to get through to the other person.

Consider the things you tell yourself and how you face the world when you communicate both internally to yourself and externally to others.

Life is a never ending journey and there's really no place to "get to." You're there right now, just like Dorothy was already home in the *Wizard Of Oz*. All she ever had to do was click the heels of her red shoes.

Isn't it amazing how some days you feel so low, and then other days you feel on top of the world? Wherever you are, how well connected you feel and how much peace within is all that matters. The cast of characters you encounter along the way will only see what you see in yourself; and, if some people are not kind to you, or choose not to see the best you have to offer, let that be their loss and not your anguish. At the same time learn from those experiences without being self-critical. Life actually becomes more fun when self-observation doesn't have to include self-judgment.

Now, let's find out how bits of anger, hurt or insecurity grow and turn hard and crusty and then fossilize over the years. If you're ready to plunge into new ideas and suggestions for dealing with your everyday crazy-making situations, read on!

6

PERSPECTIVES ON ANGER

nger is expressed in a variety of ways. If unchecked, it can negatively affect your physical as well as mental health. It can also make a situation worse. Some people explode at the slightest provocation; others direct their anger inappropriately toward someone who may have little or no role in the issue, and there are those who never seem to express anger at all.

How do you handle your anger? Do you find yourself getting mad time after time, expressing it in ways that actually make your life worse rather than better? Maybe you tend to blame others for issues that are really yours. Maybe you're the nice guy right up until you explode, because you have been trying too hard to avoid confrontations.

If you express your anger (or better yet, your feelings) directly toward the "original" source, the better your chances are of getting over it. In some cases, it is often best to express your feeling toward someone (especially one in authority, who may misunderstand you) by first writing it down. For example, expressing your anger to your boss in a letter you never send is better than taking your frustration out on your wife. You may even decide it's time to change jobs.

COGNITIVE STRESS MANAGEMENT SCALE FOR ANGER

The Cognitive Stress Management CSM scale for anger was devised to keep us more in touch with our feelings and to help us deal with them assertively, sooner rather than later. It's important to stay as close to the top of the scale as possible to have "protective padding" for those days when everything seems to go wrong.

Go through the following CSM rating scale. If you are angry with someone you care about in your personal life and you are a 6 or below, go through the chattering monkeys exercise in chapter 3 to help you consider possible options so you can make changes.

If you are a 4 or less, use the Emergency Quick Think Four-Step Plan that follows the CSM section to take immediate steps to deal with your anger effectively and in a safe manner.

#10 You truly are happy most of the time, anger rarely emerges from you. If it does pop out, you can get rid of it quickly. You effectively direct your energy and work with the person or issue causing your upset. Because you handle your feelings very well, those around you project empathy and may even positively alter their own behavior and attitudes.

Key Phrases—Honest and open; respectful to yourself and others; direct; not holding grudges; you have insight about whether the anger you feel relates to what just happened or if it was triggered by a situation or person that pushed old buttons. You make a point of learning what you can about your angry moment, and you view it as an opportunity to gain insight into yourself.

#9 Although you may occasionally get upset, you can calm yourself down. You can admit to yourself and others that you went overboard in your response, if necessary. Like a 10 on the scale, you can usually feel when an eruption is coming and you address the issue within yourself or with the other person before it comes to a head.

Once in a while you are too hard on yourself and/or others in an angry-making situation. You find it hard to forgive yourself for getting into the dilemma in the first place.

Key Phrases—Usually assertive, but occasionally defensive or non-demonstrative; may get angry later, but not for long; able to forgive and go on; well aware of your vulnerabilities so you are not too often caught off guard.

#8 Life is "good," at least for now. You feel you either have your anger in check or you don't get mad often. In fact, you handle the curve balls life throws you with a good sense of humor most of the time. However, you are sometimes overly concerned about what could go wrong in the future. Oddly enough, you may occasionally get angry just thinking about situations or people who push your buttons, even if nothing has happened in a while.

You sometimes have moments of anger about old family issues, adult relationships that have gone awry, or current global affairs such as taxes or the horrible housing market where you live. Don't underestimate the importance of maintaining a healthy diet and taking vitamins.

Key Phrases—Feeling good for the most part, but harboring anger about some parts of your life which may include memories of unresolved problems; occasional fear about possible events or situations that haven't yet happened.

#7 At times you have an angry temper and you know it. Generally, you aren't impossible to live with, but sometimes you overreact more than you care to admit to yourself or others. Those who are close to you may mention your temper.

You know you're a 7 when you have to explain yourself occasionally or compare yourself to other people by saying, "My temper isn't so bad. Look at that person over there. He really blows up."

Key Phrases—Some people and issues set you off; it takes you longer than others to become calm; mostly easy-going, but others are aware of your occasional angry flareups.

#6 You know your temper is a problem on some level, but you may not always be aware of it. In fact, you may go about life trying to convince yourself that you are under self-control. However, some situations and people tend to rile you more than you care to admit.

You may want to seek professional help in assertiveness training or anger management before things get any worse. Maybe you overreact to misdirected but well-intentioned comments. Perhaps you hold everything in and then blow-up when you come to a brick wall. Either way, there is potentially an imbalance somewhere, and it's best to address it before you go lower on the scale and experience repercussions that will get you into even more trouble.

Key Phrases—More frequent feelings of anger; outbursts of temper; deep-seated problems interacting with people; a tendency to apologize or explain your attitude, words or actions; and a need to hide anger at times.

#5 You're angry, and the color you see is red. Because you feel you have been wronged, your feelings of anger don't go away. You can't get over the other person's unreasonableness. You either are mad at yourself and wish you could go back and redo things or you can't believe someone did this to you, or both.

Whatever the case, it's important to discover your role.. Could you have avoided the angry and crazy-making situation, or were you caught in a no-win dilemma where nothing could have prevented it? If you can learn from the situation, then you can possibly avoid being set up in the future.

Key Phrases—Angry much of the day; feeling victimized or like a scapegoat; unforgiving or hard on yourself, or convinced the other guy is completely wrong. You often find it hard to stay calm in your present predicament and you feel justified in being as angry as you are.

#4 Number 4 is where your anger really begins to control you. You either turn inward with depression or outward with aggressiveness. Often, it is both, and can depend on whether or not those around you are willing to take the heat.

Recognize that both types of behaviors can be signs of hopelessness and depression. You may be experiencing low temper impulse control, where almost anything can set you off, including a mess your spouse forgot to clean up or getting cut off in traffic. Fighting, shouting, using venomous language, throwing things, and struggling with concentration or sleep may be all too commonplace.

You may fall back into old, regressive behaviors or slip into depression, drugs, alcohol or domestic violence. It's time to improve your life positively rather than focus your energy on lashing out at others.

If you're down to a 4, you're losing energy. You may not be able to make the best decisions. If you are losing hope, let others give you support. It could be good too, to get professional help to deal with your anger.

Key Phrases—Losing control of yourself and perhaps trying to control others; too hard on those who have been critical of you, especially those close to you or others who may be mistreating you and putting you down. You may respond by hurting others. Misusing drugs or alcohol could add to your problems.

#3   Almost everyday is chaos. You may be experiencing extreme anger at being fired, dropped by a lover, losing your house, or thinking your spouse is having an affair.

You may be feeling old pains of sexual, mental or physical abuse or neglect. Severe jealousy, hate, and feelings of revenge may be flooding your mind.

Whether you are reopening old wounds or experiencing new ones, your anger is turning into a rage that could seriously hurt you or someone else. If you're down to this level, you are probably incapable of seeing how current situations may be triggering old hurts you have never directly confronted.

If you are devising ways to make the pain stop or ways to get back at someone, stop and step back. Avoid the temptation to hurt yourself or others as much as possible. It is advisable to get help now, perhaps from a recommended psychiatrist.

Take care of yourself and reduce your activities to those that are calming, supportive, and may even help you physically relax and focus so you can find some balance. Don't let a downward spiral take on the momentum of a tornado and push you even lower.

Key Phrases—Volatile and out of control; feeling overwhelmed and pushed beyond your limit; losing sight of your options and believing your only choice has to be drastic; feelings of guilt or hopelessness; feeling stuck and attacked.

#2 Everyday is chaos. Everything and everyone aggravates and annoys you to the point of distraction. Even those people who are trying to ease the stress and pain in your life can't really console you. When they try to help, you become even more angry and feel more alone and misunderstood. At this level, you may be so angry and unforgiving toward yourself and or others, you could become abusive and self-destructive.

Because this is a potentially dangerous number on the scale, get support from others now—friends, professionals, your church, God, 12-step programs and other resources—before you take your anger out on yourself, someone else or both.

As a 2 on the scale, ensure all potentially dangerous drugs and loaded weapons are out of the house. Stay in a safe environment. Ask a nearby friend whom you trust to be on call.

Key Phrases—Scared; frightened; aggressive; believing there are no options; setting yourself up for things to go wrong. Life may feel so bad, you may think you are watching a terrible movie.

#1   This is the bottom line! You may feel that you have to end the pain now, and you don't care how big the price is later. This mental state is ripe for making grave mistakes. Remember doing nothing is better than doing something impulsive. Get help and support NOW before you have no recourse.

Key Phrases—Down to the raw, bottom line; feeling you have no alternatives except immediate drastic action towards yourself or others, and believing you are justified to do something now, something that can't wait.

EMERGENCY "QUICK THINK" FOUR-STEP PLAN FOR EXPRESSING YOUR ANGER EFFECTIVELY AND IN A SAFE MANNER

STOP AND TAKE A BREATH...BECOME PART OF THE POSITIVE AND SAFE SOLUTION, NOT PART OF THE PROBLEM. There is nothing wrong in feeling angry. It's how you handle your anger that's important.

Here is a four-step plan to help you assertively and positively deal with your angry feelings.

1. STEP NUMBER ONE—Repeat positive and calming self-statements NOW, such as "I'll get through this OK. Nothing is worth my making it worse."

Since your anger has been triggered, and you are probably out of control, stop everything. This is not the time to prove a point. Take time to talk yourself down. Take deep breaths slowly. Count to ten. Or, perhaps take a walk outside.

2. STEP NUMBER TWO—Save your energy and curb your feelings. In many anger-provoking situations it's necessary to emotionally take time out before you reach your limit. Don't keep trying so hard. If your expectations for your work or your relationships are too high, you may have become too emotionally involved, losing all control. Then when these high expectations are not met, you may become angry and feel abandoned and have the desire to take drastic action. Although it's easier said than done, take an "emotional vacation." Don't saturate yourself in disappointment. You are not as alone or without options as you think you are.

3. STEP NUMBER THREE—Tell yourself you have a choice in how you respond. You do have a choice about how to express your anger or whether or not you want to display your anger. Have you ever opened your eyes in the morning and thought, "This is going to be a great day," and it was? You can do likewise with anger. Tell yourself, "If I feel angry today, I'll let myself feel the pain and possibly get hurt, but I don't have to react with razor blade words; I have choices."

If an anger-provoking confrontation with someone occurs, without making excuses for others, try to resist the temptation to take the situation personally. This person may be this way with everyone. For example, you might say, "Jack must be having problems at home to behave in this manner, so I'll ignore his actions today. This isn't about me; it's about him." Or, you might say, "Jack's poor attitude has gone on too long and it's making me angry. It's time to discuss this with our supervisor."

If you are very angry at someone with whom you have an intimate relationship, you might consider that this person had no intention of upsetting you. Perhaps he or she had other issues or problems which led you to misinterpret the conversation.

4. STEP NUMBER FOUR—Calm down enough to manage the situation. Then, and only then, make a plan and follow through.

When you feel calmer, think back to what happened from as many views as possible. Try, too, to get an understanding of the big picture. Set a goal of having less stress in your life. NO act that ultimately damages your life emotionally and/or legally is worth the price you'll pay for immediate relief.

Breakups and sudden changes in relationships are hard to predict; however, you must be aware that some people and/or situations make you very vulnerable. Step out from these environments as needed.

Keep in touch with where you are on the Cognitive Stress Management rating scale, and go through the chattering monkeys exercise if need be.

How Anger Manifests Itself

Often anger manifests when you feel misunderstood or are blamed for something you feel you did not do. Anger may make you feel indignant. These powerful feelings don't just disappear. Often people suppress their anger and it surfaces later. Generally speaking, people express short-fused, suppressed, repressed or displaced anger. Study the following points for further insights and see if you relate to any of them or know anyone who fits these descriptions.

Short-fused Anger

Short-fused anger results from allowing your feelings to get out of proportion to the situation. When you experience short-fused anger, you may feel your heart pounding, and you may be unable to focus on anything but the indignities you feel you have suffered. The chattering monkeys are shouting reasons why you should be angry at the other person or situation.

Anger can overwhelm you like a powerful virus. You may not even realize how close to the surface it really is or, you may not be aware of what can trigger it. Keep in mind, however, that there are ways you can effectively handle your anger.

If you know you have a short fuse always ready to blow, explore your options immediately. You *always* have options. (Your short fuse can be a habit or perhaps has become a part of you from following the example of others. It may also be brought about by intense stress, or biochemical issues which you may not even realize you have.)

THE CASE OF FLIPPANT SERVICE MAN
The story of Scott, a friendly, well trained and competent service

man for an appliance repair store, shows how short-fused anger can damage one's job or career.

Scott, who had done well in high school, saw the appliance repair job as a good foot-in-the-door opportunity into the company. He was well liked, trusted and respected in town; he was generally easy-going and good humored and had a good driving record.

One particular day, however, he was feeling depressed because the night before his girlfriend had suggested that they see less of each other.(When he looked back, he realized he had been very moody and had been drinking quite heavily.)

As he pulled out of a driveway in his truck and turned right, another driver cut him off then honked his horn at Scott. In a gesture of anger, Scott stuck his left hand out the window and flipped his middle finger at the other driver.

It turned out to be a big mistake. Scott had forgotten the prominent sign on the back of his truck in large black letters:

**If you notice the driver of this vehicle driving unsafely or discourteously, please call
1-800-YOR FIRD**

When he returned to the shop at lunchtime, Scott was summoned into his boss' office and was told that someone had called about an incident. Scott turned red. While Scott blamed the driver for cutting him off, his boss sat quietly and listened. Then, very calmly, he said, "Scott, your presence in this community and your work for this company requires that you behave in a respectable manner at all times, and you must always act as though the customer or another driver is always right. I have noticed other discourteous behavior on your part, so this incident only solidifies my feelings. I can no longer trust you to control your temper, so I'm letting you go."

Scott was fired—as the sign on the service repair truck had warned.

Initially, Scott was angry at his girlfriend who upset him, then he was angry at the driver who had reported him, and finally he turned his anger to his boss who had fired him. But later, after some soul-searching, he realized he was responsible for his own actions. His bad mood and wounded ego had cost him a job.

Repressed And Suppressed Anger

If you experience a momentary surge of indignity but immediately hide the emotion from yourself and everyone else, usually out of fear of retaliation and rejection, you are suppressing your anger.

You may be known as the easy-going type who always gives in and extends the benefit of the doubt to others. As a child, you were probably told that anger is inappropriate or bad, particularly anger directed toward a parent or sibling. So you learned to suppress your anger and this upbringing has carried over into adulthood.

There is a difference between suppressing anger and repressing it. If it is suppressed, you know it's there. You may be gritting your teeth and clenching your fists, holding in the rage, but only you are aware of it. If anger is repressed, it becomes unconscious, and you may not even realize when you are mad. Repressed anger is bound to emerge when you least expect it or want it to happen. It results from not resolving issues and continually suppressing your anger, sometimes when you are not even aware you are doing so.

You have probably learned on a deep level that anger brings abandonment and feelings of loneliness. And, if you are fearful of rejection, here's what your chattering monkeys may be saying:

"You say that and you'll be history... Why do I always feel so bad?... He gets away with everything... I don't know what to do... I give up!"

If you have a need to please others, it will be difficult for you to even acknowledge or express your anger before you blow up. There's a good chance others don't even know you are how upset you are. If you bury your anger, you are eating fire. Unfortunately, anger turned outward at the wrong time may only prove your old fear of rejection but, anger turned inward will not only affect you emotionally, it will hurt you physically as well. Freud identified anger with depression. Others have written about anger resulting in ulcers, heart problems and other physical ailments.

SILENT STEVEN FINALLY EXPLODES

Here's a situation which shows how repressed anger can explode into violent behavior:

Steven was an office clerk for a large manufacturing company. His boss,

Herbert, was a ruthless tyrant who was despised by the men and women he supervised. Most of the staff talked about Herbert behind his back. Expressing anger directly to Herbert would have caused immediate dismissal. Steven, however, didn't complain to anyone about Herbert. He was the nice guy who did his job competently and seemed unaffected by his oppressive boss. When Herbert blew up and yelled at people, including Steven, Herbert's wrath seemed to roll off Steven like water off a duck's back. In fact, Steven had no conscious notion that Herbert affected him at all.

One day Steven was a few minutes late and Herbert chewed him out. For the next hour, Steven worked at his desk in saintly silence. Then, suddenly, he arose and walked into Herbert's glassed-enclosed office. Everyone watched in amazement as Steven, with no warning, slammed his fist into Herbert's jaw. The tyrant flew backwards, knocked over his chair and landed on the floor.

Steven returned to his usual equanimity. He went to his desk, cleaned it out, then silently left the office.

After this incident, Steven could not believe what he had done. To him it had seemed that someone else took possession of him and committed this aggressive act.

Actually, Steven had gone through his life so far removed from his own feelings he was numb. Steven had repressed his family's past criticism and rejection. He had also stifled his feeling about others who had put him down. When he couldn't hide his feelings anymore or hold any more anger, he snapped and directed all his rage toward Herbert.

Steven lost his job after this incident and became depressed and reclusive for a long time. Finally, he checked into a psychiatric hospital after a relative found him sitting listlessly in seclusion. He was given appropriate medications and was helped by a psychiatrist and a therapist who encouraged him to participate in group therapy. Later, he enrolled in a mental health center, and his life began to improve when he started to locate and acknowledge the feelings which he had repressed for so long.

Had Steven been able to stay in touch with his feelings and gone for help sooner, he probably would have learned how to release some of his frustration by talking to his co-workers. He could have sought the help of a "safe" person to talk to about his boss, and he may have filed a grievance report against Herbert or looked for another job. (Although filling a grievance seems like a good idea, it's best to check the political climate to see if it would be to your benefit. Companies have formal grievance procedures, but the reality is there are many times when no action is taken to remedy the situation.)

Displaced Anger

Another reaction to anger is to displace it. You may be able to control your feelings at the time, but they appear later when you consciously or unconsciously feel less threatened about expressing yourself. Your anger is simply waiting for a time to burst forth. Unfortunately, it can be directed to a person you love and need in your life. For example, you may get angry at your boss then go home and take it out on your spouse or children.

Sometimes anger is focused on social issues or causes instead of people. You may pick up global torches to carry and project them out into the world, feeling fully justified and supported in doing so. It's one thing to join a worthy cause that has positive meaning to you. It's quite another if your true motivation, consciously or unconsciously, is to displace anger and hurt onto an issue where you become myopic and extremist about it. So many groups and social causes are started and maintained by people who have their own axes to grind. Without realizing their motives, many people join causes to release their own buried anger, and by doing so incite other people's anger to ignite. A person may be storing a lot of burning anger from past incidents because he couldn't get away with expressing anger toward parents, siblings, spouses or others.

If you find yourself becoming upset and distraught to the point of extremism when an individual or a group has a different view point from you, you have probably become too one-sided on the issue. If you want love and justice in the world, first deal with the battles in your own mind and heart. If you feel passionately positive about some things and intense hatred about other things, you are probably displacing your anger. Your feelings are out of balance, and without balance there can be no inner peace from which to view life's issues clearly.

THE PLIGHT OF A LOYAL FRIEND...or
Fighting The Wrong Battles

Often anger is revealed when you feel strongly impelled to defend or support someone. Understandably, it is justified and even helpful in many cases. Unfortunately, getting angry in the defense of friends, co-workers, bosses and family members, may cost people jail time or in some cases, their lives. The following example shows how William got into trouble by venting his anger toward the police when they grabbed his friend.

One evening, William and a few friends from his basketball team were having a party. A neighbor called the police because the music was too loud and parked cars blocked access to his garage. When the police arrived, everyone scattered. Suddenly, the police had William's friend and team mate down on the ground, and William had no idea then (or later) why the police had his friend pinned down. Afraid his friend was going to be clubbed by the police, William became enraged. At the top of his lungs, William screamed at the officers. All of the policemen turned and looked at him simultaneously, then one officer grabbed and arrested him for obstructing justice. He spent the night in jail with his friend who got mad at him because he actually had made the situation worse.

"I couldn't stand what was going on a minute longer," William said. "I thought my friend would have appreciated my efforts. I didn't realize how it only got us into more trouble. "Everyone else involved in the noisy party had fled. I didn't really have to save the day. No one expected it."

Before you decide to jump in to help out a friend in a rash manner, try to think ahead and consider the outcome for both of you. Don't give into the heat of the moment. It may not be easy, but sometimes you truly do have to make the tough decisions about which battles to fight and which battles to walk away from. The more self-esteem you have, the less likely you will put yourself into the "I have to save-the-day role." You will have enough sense of self not to get entangled in situations that could threaten your own life or career.

In the following example, Chuck, a high school student, defended his friend at the expense of his own reputation.

One day at school John vandalized school property between classes. He was caught and taken to the principal's office. The principal and vice-principal were in the process of expelling him when John's friend Chuck got word of what was going on. Chuck felt it was his duty to defend his friend. He walked into the office and announced that not only had he vandalized the school with John, it was, in fact, his idea.

John had been sitting in a corner of the room and stared at Chuck and asked, "What are you doing?"

Chuck expected John to be happy and admire him for his false testimony, but John just responded by being surprised. Chuck ended up just hurting himself. The principal believed Chuck's story and expelled both boys. And to make matters worse, John didn't want to talk to Chuck, and in fact, tried to stay away from him. Chuck, in turn, felt rejected by his friend.

Chuck went through life for some time taking the rap for people. He didn't understand that his self-sabotaging method of playing the underdog hero was a destructive path to travel. He needed to learn to think about his own life, which unfortunately, didn't seem worthwhile to him.

Emotional Places Where Anger Takes Root

Anger often emerges when you put a great deal of effort, energy and expectation into a person or situation, and it doesn't give back what you thought it should.

Anger can come from many different sources including childhood abuse, neglect, resentment, intrusive intuition (explained later), or just extreme sensitivity.

There are a number of physical and biochemical conditions which can also provoke anger. If you have problems with anger, it is important to take into consideration your emotions and condition of your physical body. Medical tests (including brain scans) may be helpful. Physical pain and misuse or side effects of alcohol and other drugs sometimes contribute to anger. If your temper is acting up and you are on medications, contact your doctor.

Anger can also emerge from being married or being single because both of these states often remind us in seemingly harsh ways that while there may or may not be a spouse in our life, we are really basically alone within ourselves. Also, other people can't always meet our expectations, and they will disappoint us at some time or another, and likewise, we will disappoint them.

Abuse And Neglect

Abused people generally fall into four categories: (1) those who view themselves as victims of past and/or present abuse; (2) those who do not perceive that they were abused; and (3) those who feel that their abuse wasn't as bad as other people's, so they discount it; (4) and those who have healed from abuse.

Neglect is a form of abuse, and it is often underestimated. Adults who didn't have their needs met in childhood (whether physical or emotional), often have difficulty with relationships. They often demand more attention and love than can possibly be given. They need to face the past abuse, leave it behind and move forward.

If you fit into any of these categories, you are possibly continuing your history of abuse. Negative things that happened in your life may have been subtle or maybe they weren't even intentionally directed at you. No matter, they can still hurt you.

You could be attracting people in your life who perpetrate abuse or negative, yet familiar, patterns in your life. Or, you knowingly or unknowingly abuse or neglect others in some way. Even if you are not pointing fingers and blaming someone or something for your problems, you may be attracting the negativism you have come to expect. To deal with past angers from abuse, there doesn't have to be blame or judgment. It's more a matter of facing the experience of what happened, gaining insight from it, working through it, letting it go and moving on. (So often, easier said than done!)

If you have been abused at any time in your life, especially sexually, you are encourage to read the book *Courage to Heal* by Ellen Bass and Laura Davis. The authors convey great compassion and depth while helping the abused face the pain of their past to lessen their pain in the future.

The anger that comes from abuse is complex, and it has many ways of manifesting. Many people don't even realize they were badly mistreated and pass on similar types of abuse to others; some become overly responsible and resent it; while others express anger inappropriately, but feel justified in doing so.

Many abuse and neglect victims spend their lives acting as though the abuse they received as youngsters was OK or didn't happen. They may explain their treatment as appropriate discipline or something they deserved. These people generally have the attitude that "My parents taught me that life is tough, and to make it, I have to pull myself up by my own boot straps."

There are abuse victims who become anxious, uptight and overly responsible for everyone else to the point of doing a disservice. These "pathologically generous" people go so overboard, they make others feel uncomfortable.

Other abuse victims spend their lives being inappropriately angry at people and situations that don't call for such anger. They may be unaware that they need to let off steam, and they generally take it out on people or release it in situations where they think they can get away with it. They may even feel justified in being angry. Somehow, they never express their feelings about the original abuse issue, probably because it's too scary or painful to face.

At this point, you may be wondering if you have any angry residue from having been abused or neglected as a child. Can you find yourself in any one of the following scenarios?

❋ You've gone through life OK, but recently you can't take friends kidding around with you, or you get upset when people don't take you seriously. Your good humor is disappearing. Almost everything in your life is becoming some kind of issue. Your moodiness is bringing you to the point of losing friends, alienating your spouse and pushing your own children away. You feel as though you want to make up for past hurts, but you don't know how and you aren't clear about what those hurts are. All you know is you feel lonely and disconnected; and you don't know how to begin to rewire your emotional short circuits.

❋ You make plans and goals for yourself, and somehow everything seems to get botched up just as you think you might be getting somewhere. Others appear to be doing fine, but you feel like everything you touch ultimately goes wrong. Deep down you wonder if everyone else deserves to succeed but you. (Remember, this may not only be due to emotional issues or having been abused. You may be suffering from a physical/biochemical issue such as Attention Deficit Disorder.)

Many people overcome past abuse and neglect; others wallow in it forever. Although you may not be aware of your choices and options, you only keep the pain alive if you continue to live a less than happy life. Consider the case of Anthony.

ANTHONY FINALLY EMERGES FROM HIS PAST

Anthony, a successful man in his 30's, came from a complex and hurtful family who were emotionally abusive and neglectful. His father who thrived on giving "constructive criticism never let Anthony forget his mistakes. Although his parents were both successful in their own businesses, they were not successful as parents. While they didn't technically get a divorce, they were married to their jobs rather than to each other. Anthony's mother found her self-esteem through her work like his father, and Anthony was all but forgotten by his father because of his dad's business travel and desire to spend time with "important people."

Anthony's memories of his childhood were excruciatingly lonely and humiliating. His father never missed an opportunity to criticize Anthony and his mother and often ended his tirade with "You'd better watch it or you'll turn out just like your mother!" Anthony's mother had the same to say about his father. Anthony's father was too busy to be a dad, and his mother avoided him. He had little companionship with his two siblings, as they were much older than he.

"I became angry and cynical, not trusting anyone, especially those claiming to be family," said Anthony. "But I promised myself when I finished business school, I would make a life for myself, one that would put me on the inside."

Although Anthony did go through a rough adolescence, he later married a very supportive woman he met after he attended business school. She has created a safe place where he feels he really belongs. Today, he is a successful retail entrepreneur who looks at his career from a healthy perspective. While his job is important, it isn't the only thing that matters. His wife's warm, close-knit family have included and welcomed him, and at last he has a sense of being "on the inside."

He finally let go of his old label as a rejected outsider; he has come to accept love even though it was initially unfamiliar. Trusting his wife's love and her nearby family's immediate acceptance of him wasn't easy at first, but Anthony finally let the love in. He got over being jealous of his wife's close friends and close family ties, and after some rocky periods, he finally let his new family into his life.

"When my old angers surface, I go outside and run," he said. "My wife won't put up with me if I try to take my bad mood out on her. I also got into some psychotherapy when I realized I needed help in relating to those close to me. Besides, I figured, why should I let the past ruin the rest of my life?"

Resentment

Resentment is the result of doing for others and not doing enough for yourself. You end up feeling angry toward others because you feel you are doing too much for them and are not getting much back. (Generally, people don't really treat us any better than we treat ourselves.) Many experts claim that resentment can cause varous types of physical illnesses, even cancer. It has been called the fire of anger smoldering inside. "Resentment that is long held can eat away at the body and become the disease we call cancer," says

Louise Hay in her book, *You Can Heal Your Life*.

Deepak Chopra, author of *Ageless Body, Timeless Mind*, mentions a study done at Yale in 1987: "...M. R. Jensen found that breast cancer spread fastest among women who had repressed personalities, felt hopeless, and were unable to express anger, fear, and other negative emotions. Similar findings have emerged for rheumatoid arthritis, asthma, intractable pain, and other disorders."

Resentment can creep around you like ivy growing and attaching itself to a wall. At first it can seem like a wreath of protection and comfort, especially if you have pretended to forgive someone you love and care for even though they treated you like a doormat. But after decades of resentment, you begin to hate instead of love and feel choked off from happiness. Then anger can take hold, and you can find yourself alternating between quietly seething inside and having angry outbursts.

Intrusive Intuition

Anger often has a way of popping up in the wrong place at the wrong time, whether it's toward someone you don't like or don't know, or toward someone who is especially close to you. You don't have to be fighting or arguing to have your anger triggered. You may become incensed when someone tries to enlighten you, even if she has sincere, positive intentions.

Someone may also trigger your anger by giving you constructive criticism, but in reality it may have to do more with that individual's hang-ups than yours.

For instance, Susan experienced this type of anger when her mother "innocently" told her on the phone that she appeared to be gaining weight.

"Sweetheart, your extra weight could make you less sexually attractive to your husband. You know how men are. He could end up looking for and finding another woman," she said.

Susan became furious and hung up on her mother. For days she seethed inside, becoming so angry she threw one of her favorite China pieces against the wall, smashing it into a million pieces. Susan sobbed as she picked up the small bits of glass, then looked at herself in the mirror. She had indeed gained weight. She remembered how her husband Jeff no longer complimented her on how she looked in her clothes. She decided to go on a diet.

Nonetheless, Susan did not want to hear about weight problems from her mother—who was, by the way, 250 pounds. Susan was also upset with herself for acting so emotionally, reacting with hurt then blazing anger.

This type of situation could be called "intrusive intuition." Susan's mother was unconsciously tuned into her daughter's inner thinking. Instinctively, mom knew Susan did not want to look at her weight, as mom did not want to look at her own weight problem. Somewhere in mom's subconscious mind she was saying, "I want you to hate your fat just like I hate mine. I want you to feel the way I do. I want to focus on your problems and ignore my own."

At the same time, she might have felt guilty that Susan's heaviness may have come from her side of the family. Mom may have worried that Susan would be rejected as she had been. Susan was already uptight about her weight and she didn't want to face the issue. Tuning into your feelings is no small feat, particularly if it has been painful or unsafe to do so in the past.

What could Susan have done instead of staying angry and causing herself such misery? She could have honestly expressed herself, saying, "You know, Mom, that hurts. I'll work on this problem myself, but at the moment your comments are not welcome or helpful." Her mother may have gotten huffy, but Susan might have avoided being devastated and kept her self-esteem by being assertive. A little humor or acknowledgment about both of them being overweight may have helped, such as, "Mom, why don't we both go to an Overweight Anonymous meeting?" Of course, if you can make a comment like this, it shows you are tuned into your own vulnerabilities and also know how to put your ego aside when someone goes for the jugular. That's not easy, especially when you are faced with an issue you feel you are not ready to deal with yet.

It takes practice, but admitting to yourself that you've been hurt can prevent your hurt from turning to rage later. It takes time and a willingness to feel pain. It also requires an understanding that facing the pain now will save more hurt and angry outbursts later.

Getting Your Buttons Pushed In Sensitive Areas

Feeling anger toward someone may be the result of negative feelings you've carried inside for a long time. Somehow this person evokes your anger seemingly on purpose. You are dealing with "Pushing Your Buttons" anger. Now's the time to become familiar with what your old buttons are.

Knowing that your anger is a held-over energy may not make it easier for you to deal with this person, but it could turn your dilemma into an opportunity. If you recognize the issues you are sensitive about, you can decide to work on them, see them for what they are, and let them go, or at least steer clear of the person or situation that evokes them as much as possible, at least for now.

If someone continually "invites" you to be angry, think about the buttons he may be pushing. They often represent issues you already had inside long before this individual ever showed up. Look at this person with a fresh new view and determine if he reminds you of someone or some feeling in your past, perhaps someone in your family. You may have unconsciously drawn this person or situation into your life because you are still working out an old issue. Amazingly, you may be magnetized to a new face that represents an old situation. Maybe you are being used as a scape-goat or exploited in some way.

Make use of your experience. Decide whether you want to confront the situation by standing up for yourself in an assertive manner, overlook it, or just walk away. Whatever you choose, it's your decision. The eye-opener for this experience is that you have made your own choice, a choice that you may not have had in your past scenario, especially when you were a child.

The Anger Of Being Married

Being intimately close to someone for a long period of time can set the stage for all types of emotions, anger being one of them. No situation can bring out anger in deep personal ways like marriage, especially if you have been holding on to past wounds. (In fact, anger in a marriage can bring out the worst in people. Police officers have been known to say they would rather deal with almost any other type of case than a domestic violence problem.)

Think of the couples you know. How many of them really have happy marriages? There are a great number of people who have been, are, and will be involved in happy, successful love and marriage relationships. Perhaps you are one of them. No doubt, however, for a number of couples under the veil of apparent marital bliss, there may be deceptions of happiness. Once the initial flame of passion and the feeling of being in love diminishes, the marriage partners may ask, "Is this all there is?" "Can I take this any more?" Maybe the wife gave up her lifelong dreams for the financial security her husband appeared to have offered, and visa versa. Perhaps she married to cure her loneliness or because this man was better than anyone else she had met. Maybe the husband sticks around because his wife will "take him to the cleaners" if he leaves her. Maybe they're both "hanging in there for the children."

Perhaps jealousy, insecurity and the fear of being left alone flame the potential fire of anger. Whatever the situation, many couples find themselves caught up in being angry about their marriage. Consider Ellen and Bob's scenario.

ELLEN AND BOB'S LOST YEARS

When Ellen married Bob 17 years ago, mostly for reasons of security and physical attraction, she had him wrapped around her finger. Over the years, she realized that she stayed with her husband, whom she thought she didn't really love, for more than financial need and a sense of security. She also was emotionally tied to him. Deep down, she had a fear of being rejected or deserted if she ever cared deeply for someone. For this reason, Ellen gave great importance to always having the upper hand.

Ellen, an educated woman, was very involved in an absorbing part-time job while raising their two children. The rest of her life was also very busy and full, which left little time for Bob. This gave Ellen her pseudo sense of control, but in reality, it kept her from attaining the joy of intimacy and trust she desperately craved.

Bob wrapped himself tighter and tighter in the soft cocoon of his recliner and TV remote control. As time went on, he became numb to his feelings of loneliness. His family was a cold one, but he didn't recognize it as such.

Ellen and Bob's resentment toward each other culminated one evening when Ellen and her son were in the kitchen laughing loudly. Bob left the TV to see what was going on, and they appeared to laugh even louder as he came into the room. Bob wondered if they were laughing at him, and he envied the apparent bond they had between them. Ellen and her son interacted in a carefree manner; they had none of the awkwardness Bob and Ellen had in their marital relationship.

Bob stood watching for a couple of minutes then stepped out of the room. He seethed inside. Then for the first time in years, he decided to take action. He turned off the television and walked back to the kitchen. Bob's anger exploded as he looked at Ellen, "How come you never laugh that way with me?"

Ellen looked at him blankly, realizing she had numbed her own emotions over time, finding it increasingly more of a joy to be with her son than to be with her husband. As they sat later in the living room in silence, neither one knew what to say to the other. After a few futile attempts to discuss the situation, they eventually decided to get some counseling as it might be the only way to improve their relationship.

Few things are as angry making as feeling stuck or frighteningly vulnerable in a relationship. Hopeless relationship situations can mentally distort each partner's perspective on life and can even lead to physical ailments. Don't ruin your life. You and your family deserve more.

If you have been below a 7 on the CSM scale for anger for a long time in your adult relationship, get help before the anger fully takes hold and destroys the ties you have with this person.

Even if you are married, read over the next section, *The Anger of Being Single*. Much of the material included in this section touches on the pain of marriage and cuts through some of the anger so you can perhaps rethink your perspective and try to rediscover each other. Often those who are married are envious of those who are single and vice versa. The sad reality is that we tend to be consumed with the idea that there is someone special or some better situation waiting for us out there, when in reality that someone "better" is actually inside us waiting to be discovered.

The following poems don't represent all male and female relationships. Both poems are merely a reflection on how a woman and man might feel if they are angry or hurt in a situation and can only see it from a dependent person or victim's point of view. (We would all do well to remember it takes two to tango. We should all find ways to empower ourselves. In the long run, we will help each other.)

About To Sing The Bag Lady Blues

Clutching my resume close to my heart,
I wince at my leaning on some man who's "smart."
He may feed my stomach, but starved is my soul.
I seem to keep waiting to fill up this hole.
Do I have it in me to go it alone?
Would that make me happy? Would I starve to the bone?

I see myself standing out on Route 10
With a sign that is written with some cast off pen:
"I'll sing for my supper if you take me in.
I'll pretend to be happy. I'll try to stay thin.
I'll say that I love you. I'll act like I'm thrilled.
I'll sigh with relief when it's you that gets billed."

I'll sit in my backyard. I won't move away.
Afraid I'd be a bag lady with no home one day.
I know that I'm "safe" here. That's good for a start.
But what do I do about my homeless heart?
Is it that I'm lazy? Am I sad inside?
He can't make me happy. From myself I can't hide.

I know it's not his job. I'll do it on my own.
But must I be lonely when I'm not alone?
Is life possible with him? Should I seek someone new?
Is this part of our journey or are we just through?
It's dumb to think happiness comes from a man.
I'll do it for me now. I know that I can.

I'll focus myself more. I'll find my own bliss.
I'll make myself whole whether "Mrs." or "Miss."
Yet I need to know somehow which way it should be.
The truth is this worry keeps me from being me.
How can I be certain that I want to stay,
If it's because I fear horror if I go away?

I wish my own dad had been there for me more,
So I don't hold a man tightly to settle the score.
How come when I wonder about filling my own shoes,
That I find myself singing "The Bag Lady Blues?"

Barbara Ann Berg, June 22, 1996

Can You Really Please A Woman And Still Be A Man?

I remember the days when we both talked with ease.
She didn't criticize and was easy to please.
I felt I could be honest with each word I'd say,
And not feel forced to see things all her way.

But then something happened, I do not know when.
I found myself holding back a thought now and then.
I'd say things to please her, to get through the night.
So she wouldn't get angry and then start a fight.

She says I'm lying, not telling the truth.
But if I'm real honest she goes through the roof.
She wants to talk "feelings" when we get in bed.
If I get romantic she cries or plays dead.

No subject stays simple, she beats it to death.
I storm out of the house just to catch my own breath.
She runs out to get me and have the last word.
I get on the defensive, trapped like a bird.

She rants and she raves until I start to shout.
I frankly can't take it. Seems there's no way out.
I wish that I knew what a man's supposed to do,
'Cause I feel like the loser in each fight we go through.

I swear that I'm trying the best that I can,
But the rules are all changing for being a man.
One minute the "strong" approach seems it will win.
The next, I start feeling I've got to give in.

I think I'll go nuts when she changes her moods,
because whatever I do she just ponders and broods.
Perhaps if I just say this is all my fault,
She'll back off and bring all her wrath to a halt.

So what about all of this business of "growth?"
Did I promise I'd do this when we got betrothed?
I suppose "looking inward" is good for us all,
But it just can't beat watching a good game of ball.
Can you really please a woman and please yourself too?
Or is that just on commercials regarding some brew?
I can't live without her, at least that's what I say,
But I hope she'll stop trying to change me one day.

I am who I am, and I do what I do.
Our lives will go smoother if you see that too.
I guess that you're trying the best that you can.
Don't expect so much from me, I am only one man.

Barbara Ann Berg, June 30, 1996

The Anger Of Being Single

The pain of being single can be excruciating if you have never been alone for long periods of time, or if you have been alone for a while and long for someone to share your life.

If you have been alone for a long stretch, it could be that your high expectations may be keeping you from developing a new, realistic, long-term relationship. If you are looking for gold and you find silver, maybe you could take a closer look inside and go for the opportunity to find the gold in yourself.

"Star light, star bright
Where the Hell is Mr. Right?"

The above phrase on a metal car license plate cover says a lot. Note how the request is for Mr. Right rather than Ms. or Miss. Right. Although just as many men as women are in search of their perfect mate, men are less inclined to publicly acknowledge their unhappiness at being single.

Why is the state of being single so lonely and angry making? Watch almost any commercial or pick up any magazine and you'll come to believe that in our "couple's world" the perfect couple is madly in love and lives happily ever after together. Contrast that to the reality of being single, where it's hard to find someone to share a cup of coffee and conversation, much less a soul mate.

If you base your life on what you see on TV commercials and in magazines, the perfect mate has a perfect male or female body (by US standards). This person will sweep you off your feet. After months and even years of seeking this ideal, you believe that one of your inalienable rights is to find the perfect someone who's just right for you, or that you are the perfect match for the type of person you are seeking. It's no wonder you become angry.

The crux of the anger you and other singles may experience

doesn't necessarily mean your standards are too high, although they may not be realistic. Your *expectations* are too high. You want someone to be what you want the person to be, while not accepting who and how they are. In this day and age, you will bring more pain and anger into your life if you continue to put too much stock and idealistic expectations into lovers, relationships and marriage. Until you understand that you "attract exactly what you are inside," you'll continue to be angry for reasons that could distract you from ever finding yourself. The next time you meet someone, you might ask yourself, "Is this person an attraction or a distraction?"

Your hope for dealing with this type of anger lies in understanding yourself and accepting that it's not your lover's job to live up to your expectations or to make you feel alive. Perhaps you might do well to pattern your relationship with a human as you would with your pet. Fido or Fluffy don't expect much from you and you don't expect much from them; you just love them as they are.

Anger seems to arrive when you put a great deal of effort, energy, expectation, and attention in a certain direction and it doesn't come back to you in the way you thought it should. The less you struggle to be coupled in order to feel complete, the less angry you'll be. When you don't have an exact picture of what Mr. or Ms. Right will look like and do for a living, the better chance you have for success with Cupid.

Don't worry about meeting Mr. or Ms. Right. Work on becoming right for yourself. In the event you do meet the love of your life, do not give up who you really are just so you're not alone. It will only make you angry....and make you want to leave...then you'll be single again ... and angry because there's no one out there for you.

Harnessing And Working Through Your Angers

Learn to Say "No"

Are you the type of person who gives and gives until you are drained? There is a difference between giving freely and sacrificing to the point of creating resentment and crazy making for yourself.

Take steps in learning to say no, when it's what you really want to say. Initially, you may not get positive responses when you become less available, but eventually you will feel less exhausted; and you will also avoid the resentment that dependent friends or associates may harbor for desperately needing you so much. You may even gain a little respect from them now and then.

Here are a few points to consider:

* What are your true motives for saying "yes?" Is it only so others will think you are perfect even when you are overwhelmed. Instead, learn to say, "I can't do it this time, but please keep me in mind." It's a no-win situation when you work overtime to make others think you are more pliable than you really are. Bending too far will break almost anyone.

* Decide each morning when you wake up how much you can reasonably accomplish that day. If you register a 6 or below on the CSM scale for anger, be prepared to say no to anything extra thrown in your path. Just be responsible for your own

obligations. Be there for yourself first and for others when you can.

❊ Realistically tell yourself and others you must take care of your own needs if you are to be an effective spouse, employee or friend. When you feel guilty for taking care of yourself, recognize that you are only putting yourself in your own double bind, and that guilt only keeps you from finding any real peace for yourself and others in the long run.

Write A Letter To Yourself Or Keep A Journal

Whether you write the letter to yourself or to someone else, therapeutic letter writing is a safe place to vent your anger. (A therapeutic letter is one you write, but don't send.) File the letter where no one else will find it. Or, when it no longer serves a purpose, burn it or tear it up. A journal to yourself is for your eyes only, or for those who would not be judgmental and who truly understand you. Journals are wonderful for writing about all of your feelings. Here are a few thoughts about writing letters and journals:

❊ Write a therapeutic letter to the person with whom you are angry. Leave no holds barred. Either take the letter to your therapy or support group, or keep it in a safe place. Re-write the letter occasionally and read it to yourself or to someone you can trust. Writing letters can be quite effective ways to express yourself, even if you're writing to people who are deceased. The purpose is more for you to see what is truly in your own heart than to reveal information to someone else.

❈ If you are feeling angry with yourself for staying stuck or putting up with a situation too long, write a forgiveness letter to yourself.

Forgiving yourself is one of the finest acts of healing you can do. Write about the lessons you have learned and vow not to repeat the mistakes over again. However, if you do repeat the same mistakes, forgive yourself again. Life is for learning, and if no mistakes are made, no real learning takes place.

Remember the quote by Marcel Proust, "The real voyage of discovery consists not in seeking new landscapes, but in having new eyes?" Often, feelings of anger will give us new eyes, if we are willing to look at things differently and without judging them as "bad." Look at tough situations as challenges that give your life color and depth.

In his book, *God Calling God at Eventide*, A. J. Russell states:

"Life with Me is not immunity *from* difficulties, but peace *in* difficulties. My guidance is often by *shut* doors. Love bangs as well as opens."

❈ When you are experiencing anger, think of areas of your life where you can make changes for the better. Work with the anger to use it to propel you forward to a better place in life, not hold you back. Writing about both the positive and the negative aspects can be empowering, and it can widen your horizons while improving your perspective.

Begin confronting the issues or person you are angry with on paper. Be as direct as possible. Also, recognize if you directly approach that person, you may not get the response you had hoped for. Is it worth it or not? Will the person listen to you? Are there different ways to approach the issues? Perhaps it is worth it to you just to hear yourself say what you have to say to that person. Really do the best you can to make this experience a positive and winning one, not another disappointment where you feel shot down yet one more time.

Take Steps To Empower Yourself

When you are angry, empower yourself in some way. Think of something that is important to you, and don't hold back from doing it. For example, if you have been wanting to take a trip, begin making plans. If you want to go back to school, sign up. If you want to write a book, write it. Or, if you want to take tennis lessons, take them. Write down the steps you need to take to reach your goal.

Anger often comes from feeling powerless and thinking there is a lack of progress in your life. Take steps to fulfill a goal. When you achieve it, it can help dissipate a lot of your frustration.

Make sure you select something that is realistic to tackle. Be careful with whom you share your goals and don't let others tear down your plans.

In the event you are looking for a new job, begin rewriting your resume. Sometimes this requires help, insight, and encouragement from other people. This would also be a strategically good time to obtain written letters of recommendation.

Eliminate The Blame

To deal with past angers, don't focus on blaming or judging yourself or others. You can just recognize and be willing to experience the feelings of grief or sorrow for what happened, and acknowledge how you would have felt if the situation had a positive outcome. Let it go, then enjoy life a few notches up from the past negativity without repeating the same saga.

Your life story develops according to how you respond to what is said and done to you over and over. You can choose to ignore your past; but play it over and over without realizing it. You can face it for what it was, and then move on to more positive actions and situations. Or, you can consciously play the victim and wallow in the negativity for the rest of your life.

Others will see you in whatever way you see yourself. If you're angry and blaming, you probably have good reasons, but that will only bring more problems back to you. Choose now to let some hurts go and to forgive yourself and others.

Don't force or push the process faster than is realistic for you. Take all the time you need. Most importantly, make the healing and peace of mind your goals.

Learn From Your Mistakes

Make it a point to learn from your mistakes whenever possible and to objectively look at problems that come into your life. Be honest about your role in any situation, even if you don't feel at fault.

It is not necessary for one person to be good and the other bad.

In one case history, a woman was deathly afraid of her brother; however, she gained great insight when he told her one day that her nasty verbal assaults frightened him immensely.

Goethe offers this helpful line: "Never let that which is most important to you be at the mercy of that which is least important to you." Amazingly, during moments of anger, you may jeopardize your livelihood, and other vital aspects of your life, because your ego has been bruised.

If you find a way to truly experience your feelings, yet stay detached enough to not overreact, you'll be way ahead of the rest of the world. Don't let your anger justify doing and saying things you'll regret later.

In Closing

After all is said and done, anger is a response to the culmination of things that you feel impinge on your sense of dignity and survival at that moment in time. Feeling anger and using it to empower you forward, rather than letting it push you further back, is be one of the greatest feats you can accomplish in your lifetime. Overcoming your own crazy-making demons can truly help the rest of the people in the world overcome their own.

Anger seems to be something from deep within, and for many people, it sits all too close to the surface. If your anger within is a constant companion that doesn't go away and continually disrupts your life and the lives of others, take a moment and ask yourself, "OK, what can I gain from this?"

Maybe your deep-seated anger comes from never really being appreciated or understood for who you are. Unfortunately, when it comes out and is directed at other people, with no tact or forethought, you are only setting yourself up to be misunderstood and alienated once again. Sadly, our anger is often out of frustration that comes from not being able to get close to someone else. However, emotional outbursts only push people further away.

If an anger scenario keeps popping up, it will probably continue to do so until you come to understand the part you are playing in this issue and learn the lesson it has in store. All you have to do is be willing to stop and look at things in another way.

7

DISSOLVE HURT FEELINGS— DON'T BECOME A VICTIM

Hurt is one of the most raw, vulnerable and painful emotions you can experience. It can make you feel rejected, misunderstood, discounted, manipulated, ignored, discarded, abandoned, used, taken for granted, humiliated and more.

You may actually hide your hurts from yourself without ever realizing how far you go to avoid your pain. Unfortunately, the pain you suppress and bury now will get worse later, because it builds and accumulates like a growing snowball.

Oddly enough, at a time when you feel you need the greatest support, you are actually in a mindset where misunderstandings are apt to occur. If you are hurt by someone or by a group of people, for instance, it probably seems obvious and clear to you why your feelings are hurt. However, since others are involved, there will always be another point of view.

When you are hurt, you are also vulnerable to being cast into the role of a victim, a role that makes you feel sorry for yourself. Some people make a lifetime career of staying the victim, going from one hurt and disappointment to another. Ideally, most people feel their pain for a while, then after learning from the situation, they move on, trying not to get caught in the same scenario again.

It's not always easy to get over hurt, especially if your pain stems from an issue that is very sensitive to you. With or without realizing it, some issues may upset you more than others, and you are more inclined to get hurt when these issues are involved.

The gradual building of hurt, when combined with anger, avoidance, and denial, can throw you far out of balance, and professional help may be required to get you back on track. Unchecked, hurt can develop into deep resentments and regrets, estrangement from others, major depression, passive-aggressive behavior, drug and alcohol overuse and even violence.

Hurt generally precedes anger, even if you don't realize it. If you don't deal with your hurt and growing anger at the time it occurs, you may unconsciously direct it to others. You may go from denying hurt and explode into anger in less than sixty seconds, thereby making those around you feel like they need to walk on eggshells.

COGNITIVE STRESS MANAGEMENT SCALE FOR HURT

An initial step in dealing with hurt is to find out where you are on the Cognitive Stress Management scale for hurt. You may find yourself relating to several numbers at the same time, or one number in particular. Read on and decide whether you should make some assertive changes before you go lower on the scale and before the crazy-making situation gets worse.

#10 If you're a 10 on the hurt scale, you are not afraid to completely experience happiness, disappointment, pain and all. If you feel you have been wrongfully treated, you acknowledge this pain to yourself and to others when appropriate. If you get hurt or upset in a close relationship, you can admit the part you played. You are willing to make changes. If you are hurting from a major loss, you recognize that new insights are available to you down the road and you experience your pain and grief now rather than deny it.

Key Phrases—Understanding and forgiveness; ability to face pain and work it through rather than avoid it; communication with others about your pain.

#9 As a 9, you acknowledge your hurts, decide what to do about them, and go about life almost as well as a 10; the process just takes a little longer. You know that you are vulnerable and sensitive at times and your feelings do get hurt, but you don't hold a grudge. When you let others know you are hurt, you do it in a way that helps them understand your point of view.

Key Phrases—Tactful in expressing your viewpoint to others; occasionally have hurt feelings, but generally strive not to incur them.

#8 You feel good about the way you deal with hurt feelings for right now. However, you realize that if you don't create options for yourself and consider other perspectives, you could be setting yourself up to get hurt or to feel victimized later on. You may be in a friendship, job, or love relationship where you sometimes feel taken for granted, or you feel there are issues which need to be addressed.

Key Phrases—Know how to get help and support from others when necessary; not fearful of being hurt, but cautious and aware of what issues might develop; understand how to work out of pain; know when to get out of situations.

#7 At this level on the scale, you get hurt easier than those at an 8, 9, or 10. As a 7, you are generally in touch with your feelings. However, you may be inclined to say, "I shouldn't feel so upset. Look at what *that* person has to bear."

Key Phrases—Minimal avoidance of hurt; occasional tendency to take a victim's stance or feel sorry for yourself; tell yourself it's OK when it isn't.

#6 You may spend more time than you care to admit being hurt or upset with others or with the world in general. Consider what you might be doing to set yourself up for others to hurt you. Don't take a victim-like stance by going from one hurt to another or holding on to old hurts for dear life. As painful as it make be, learn everything you can from your situation, especially if you notice some patterns taking place.

Key Phrases—May be emotionally over-invested in a person or situation; inability to see beyond your own perceptions of the world; tendency to repeat old hurt patterns; have trouble forgiving yourself for succumbing to old patterns.

#5 As a 5 on the scale, you are not only hurt, but you are openly angry about why this happened to you. It can be helpful to feel this intense emotion, especially if it helps you to get in touch with what is really going on inside and if it helps you to grieve, resolve and move on. However, if your pain is directing you to get back at someone else in a vindictive way, you could be setting yourself and others up for more hurt.

Key Phrases—Tendency to project fault on others to avoid hurt; overly judgmental and critical of yourself and others; occasional irrational thinking.

#4 Your hurt could be causing you to think about little else, even causing you major depression. Because your hurt and sadness may take time to get over and your ability to think clearly and make useful decisions could be diminished, outside help and support groups may be helpful. Don't keep trying to get through it without outside help. Others may already be worried about you more than you want to acknowledge. Even more importantly, you deserve fresh insight to help you gain new perspectives.

Key Phrases—Sleeplessness and/or obsessiveness over a hurtful situation; loss of energy; a "go-it-alone" attitude; difficulty focusing on regular daily activities.

#3 You are easily hurt by others to the point that you almost always feel you are on the bottom of the pile. Others may feel they have to tiptoe when they are around you because almost anything they say or do you misunderstand and vice versa.

Key Phrases—Feeling like a scapegoat, believing others are rejecting or mistreating you; inability to see a pattern in hurtful situations; too hard on yourself; emotionally abandoned; feeling terribly alone.

#2 At the 2 level, you may be almost convinced that there isn't much you can do. The lower you go on the scale, the harder it is to view anything clearly. If this is your case, ask yourself what you can do differently. A change in attitude and expectations takes time, but it is a powerful change in the long run.

Key Phrases—Inability to let go of hurt feelings; barely able to function at all in day-to-day activities; not knowing where to turn for insight and direction.

#1 Because you are at the bottom, give yourself credit for just hanging in there. Create a holding zone for now, and know that with time and support, new options will appear. Standing back and doing nothing for the time being may be the most positive route to take. Surround yourself with as many positive people and as much loving energy as you can. You may find yourself getting help from unexpected places.

Key Phrases—Suicidal thoughts; feelings of hurting others or yourself; depressed; overwhelmed by pain; in need of major life change or experience.

Your Reality Check On Hurt

Determine where you are right now. Are you hurt? Do you feel angry? Are you upset about something you have done? Are you upset with someone else? Do you feel your life is out of control? Do you feel you are at the mercy of someone else's behavior? Are you furious with someone one week then with another person the next? Are you in an upsetting situation which only seems to be getting worse?

If you answered yes to any of these questions, go back to the watch-checking exercise in Section II, on page 112. As you check your watch every hour, ask yourself one or more of these questions:

❋ Do you entertain a mixture of feelings? What are they? How much is hurt, anger, happiness, anguish or disappointment? Notice how these emotions may mix together.

❋ Do you recognize a pattern? Do you feel hurt when you are criticized for something or not taken seriously?

❋ Does your fear of being alone uncover old wounds?

❋ Do you feel hurt when you are asked to do more tasks than you really want to? Is it because you can't say no? Are you upset because others don't set limits or boundaries for you?

❋ Do you think you should be grateful or insist on trying to make something work when you really can't?

Some of our hurts are big and obvious, hurts that would probably break almost anyone under the strain. Others hurts are subtle, or prick like little splinters in your skin which you can barely see. But you know you need to deal with them when you can't get them out of your head. Perhaps your heart is beating in fear of what could happen next. Even if you are in the middle of a crisis, attempt to discover what old fears and patterns are coming up again. There's a good chance you are safer or in a better place than you think you are. Old tapes of mistrust and panic may be coming to the forefront as you gather more stress.

How You "Set Yourself Up" For Feelings Of Hurt

As you go through the next few pages, consider how pain and hurt occur in the first place.

If You Avoid Pain Now You Will Pay Later

There are times when you may pretend a disturbing situation isn't really going on. If you avoid dealing with a dilemma head on, there is a good chance you are involved with some unfinished business, which complicates the situation.

You may be trying to forgive someone, but you can't let go of old negative feelings. And, you're having a hard time attaining a new perspective of what has happened. This indicates that true resolve or being "over it" hasn't genuinely occurred.

Even when you think you have gotten over a past hurt, you may suddenly explode with grief about it later on. In this case, you may have unconsciously covered up an old hurt with a new one.

Whether you realize it or not, you may take the path of least resistance in dealing with your hurt, sometimes in a most subtle way. Consider the following examples. Do they sound familiar?

❄ You take a new job you don't like. It's a long commute, too, but you took the job because you've experienced the pain of being rejected for employment by three other companies.

❄ You date someone who bores you to tears because it's too painful to spend Saturday nights alone.

❄ You marry someone whose infidelity during the courtship has already hurt you, but you hope that marriage will keep him or her from meandering.

❄ You know in your heart you need to work for yourself, but out of fear of the risks involved, you work for someone else and put off your lifelong dream.

❄ You allow your spouse to talk you into having his razor-tongued mother move into your home because you don't want to argue with your spouse.

✤ You stay in the family business rather than go into a career you prefer because it would upset your parents.

What do these situations have in common? They are all examples of trying to avoid pain. Think of other "wrong turns" or "overly challenging heartaches" you've experienced. What would you have done differently? What would you have done the same?

Don't beat yourself up about the past; simply learn what you can from the experience and do it differently next time. The chattering monkeys exercise in chapter 3 will help you create positive options to face your hurt feelings.

Ignoring The Warning Signs

For many reasons, it's frighteningly easy to ignore warning signs of hurt. You may have a lot invested in your job, business, love affair, friend or child care provider. You may also feel this person would be hard or impossible to replace. You may be under the impression that this person is one you can't approach about how you really feel.

For this reason, rather than deal with your hurt feelings, you rationalize to yourself that things are really fine and the potential problems will just blow away. Sometimes they do, but often they begin multiplying. The following examples of what you say, vs. the reality, show how a sense of pseudo-peace is often maintained:

✤ "I've been hurt by my father-in-law's cruel words many times. Now, my husband wants his father to move in with us, and I'll probably give in just to save a major fight with my husband." (Frankly, I don't know which is worse, listening to my father-in-law or fighting with my husband. I'll bide my time until I can figure out what to do next.)

❋ "I don't want anything to do with my ex-husband, who has hurt me with his infidelity too many times. Yet, when something breaks down, he's the one I call for help." (I know I depend on him too much even while I can't stand him. I'm hoping maybe he will change.)

❋ "I really don't like or trust this person much because he's hurt my feelings by divulging personal information to others at work. For some reason, I continue to play racquetball with him twice a week." (I don't understand what's going on; maybe, if I spend more time with him, he will respect me more and talk about me less.)

Disappointments Intertwined With Hurt

Just as you are getting over the hurt from one disappointment another follows. Does this seem to be your pattern? If so, you may be creating disappointments and hurts without realizing it. There are several ways people set themselves up for disappointments. Consider these examples.

OVERLOOKING ANNOYANCES—Joy starts dating a man who smokes, a habit she gave up ten years earlier. Although the habit bothers her immensely, she continues to date him because he is good looking and has a steady job. The key word is "overlook." The more you overlook things that are important to you, the quicker your route to disappointment and hurt. In actuality, the very thing you overlook in the beginning bowls you over in the end.

ALLOWING RIDICULE—Joe has great fun with his friend when they're out alone; however, if other people are around, Joe's friend begins making belittling comments. Joe has discussed this situation with his friend to no avail. If Joe continues this relationship, he's surely headed for more hurt feelings unless he refuses to accept the ridicule. In this case, he could wait until the situation occurs again, and in front of others say, "Why do you treat me this way now, with people around, then act so nicely when we are alone?"

MIND READING—Because Maria harbors the romantic illusion that her husband should know when she's in need of a compliment or a bouquet of flowers, she creates one disappointment after another in her marital relationship. It might be less romantic to tell people what you have on your mind, but in the long run, it's more practical and wise. Mind reading expectations are unrealistic whether it's in marriage, a friendship or a work situation. You would be wiser to say, "I'd really love to be surprised this week by receiving some flowers from you. I really need some now."

BLIND OPTIMISM—There is a big difference between genuine optimism and stoically pretending things are going well when they are not. For example, at least one aerospace engineer in his late fifties has made the mistake of thinking he was set for life in his job, even when those around him were being laidoff. He didn't update his resume or keep in touch with his networking contacts, so when his pink slip appeared, he didn't have any job prospects, and he fell into a deep depression which lasted several months.

In another example, the wife of a high-powered attorney used her blind optimism as a crutch to believe that her husband would always be around to support her, even after he had three heart attacks and two affairs. Had she developed a few marketable job skills or stayed on top of their financial situation, she probably wouldn't be in a near poverty condition today. She had relied on an undying optimism that she would always be taken care of.

True optimism includes a willingness to try new angles as you proceed ahead with a positive attitude. Hoping everything will get better if you wait long enough without taking the effort to create better chances for survival is just setting yourself up for failure. When you land at the bottom of the heap, you could end up blaming the rest of the world for your own undoing.

Don't wait until it is too late to eliminate disappointments from your life. Do what you can now to make tomorrow brighter. If there is nothing you can do, rest easy in knowing you have done all you can. There are few worse feelings in life than realizing too late all the things you could have done or should have done.

True optimism comes from resting with the knowledge that you have done all you can. It doesn't come from waiting for someone or something to come and save you from yourself.

Settling For Something Less

It's one thing to settle for living in a house that doesn't have a sunken living room, but it's quite another matter to settle for conditions that negatively affect your life, like moving your household and children to a place that feels so unsafe you are too worried about getting robbed or held up to get a full night's sleep.

Whether you realize it or not, you are making decisions every day. Often these decisions involve your entire existence; other times they just involve a choice between fish or chicken at your local restaurant.

Erik Erikson wrote that when we enter old age, we have the developmental dilemma of facing dignity vs. despair. Every day you are moving either toward dignity or despair. In which direction are you moving?

When you settle for a less than acceptable situation, you're setting your life up for hurt and pain. Living a life you can barely tolerate isn't worth living. It's only time spent waiting to die.

Beware Of The Narcissistic Personality

One of the most tragic ways to break someone's spirit or to rob him of authenticity is to never "mirror" for that person, that is to never truly listen and respond to what he is saying.

History recounts stories of many cultures where people were ostracized from their own family or community for a serious infraction or even a perceived transgression. These discarded people were often treated as though they were dead or non-existent. Not only did the rejected ones ultimately end up moving away, they often killed themselves outright. Today, for the most part, people are generally not so publicly ostracized as individuals, but many can still suffer from neglect, contempt and misunderstanding within families and society for expressing their own ideas and viewpoints others refuse to see.

Sadly, many children in our culture suffer from neglect. Their parents do not give them the attention they need and deserve. Some parents are either busy with other children, dealing with their own burdens of getting through life, or meeting their own previously unmet needs, so their children go through life without being heard. If these children exert opinions or somehow cross their parents, they are abused, shunned or completely ignored. Even without touching them, parents can violate their children by discounting or refuting what they say, ignoring their requests, minimizing their hurts and feelings, and acting as if they are not even in the room.

The story of Narcissus and Echo is an example of how you and others may go through life with unmet needs that eventually create hurt and pain.

In Greek mythology, Echo was a lovely nymph adored by many. However, she had one flaw. She talked too much. And, she always had to get the last word in. One day, Juno was searching the woods for her man, whom she was afraid was engaging in romantic activity with the wood nymphs. Echo distracted Juno from finding the nymphs so they could get away undetected.

When Juno realized what Echo had done, she put a curse on her. Echo would get the last word all right, but no one would respond to her requests and needs.

A few days later, Echo came upon the ever so handsome Narcissus, who was gazing at himself in the water. Narcissus would call out to himself, "How beautiful." Echo would repeat the same words out loud, thinking he was referring to her. Each time this happened, Narcissus would turn toward Echo, seemingly delighted in what she had to say. This attention pleased Echo greatly, and she soon fell in love with Narcissus, thinking he was in love with her.

However, when Echo talked about herself or expressed her own opinions, Narcissus would ignore her to the point that Echo soon became heartbroken. Echo finally realized that Narcissus never loved her at all; he only loved flattering words that were focused on himself.

Were you a child no one listened to? If so, you may have become a people pleaser or "Echo" willing to "kiss up" to anyone who pays attention to you, anyone who gives you more attention than you received as a child. When this happens, you may be all too willing to work harder than anyone else in the office, to put up with mean and abusive people who seem a step up in the kindness department from your parents, and to take on friends who seem to give you more attention than you are used to getting, especially when you're telling them what they want to hear.

Truly good friends have a way of taking turns being Echo and Narcissus. When you first meet someone, objectively observe your interaction. The following questions can help you determine if you are moving into a healthy relationship or a relationship that will leave you hurt and angry.

❊ Does your friend ask how YOU are doing?

❊ Does he seem to really care about you?

❊ Is he as good to you as you are to him?

❊ Does your friend take you for granted?

❊ Is he nice only when trying to win you back?

❊ Does everything seem to go your friend's way? Or are your wishes and desires considered?

❊ Is your friend able to overlook your foibles? (Hopefully, you are aware of what they are and do the best you can to effectively deal with them.)

❊ Do you continually feel you have to act as though you haven't been slighted or embarrassed by your friend?

It is important for you to decide why you select certain people and environments. Are you hanging around because it vaguely reminds you of your family and an old family issue you are reenacting and are trying to work out? Are you possibly hoping you'll get something from this relationship that you didn't get from your family? If so, you are again setting yourself up for hurt and disappointment.

Being The Monkey In The Middle

Another subtle but sophisticated slant to the Narcissus and Echo story is being the "Monkey in the Middle." Consider the case of Trudy, who appeared to be loved by everyone. She was always there if someone needed her. People could and would tell her all their problems, which made Trudy feel important.

In one particular work-related incident, Jan complained to Trudy about Lucy's poor work habits, how she was always late and how much time she spent on the telephone. Later, Lucy came to cry on Trudy's shoulder. She discussed Jan's arrogant attitude and described the difficulties she had working with her.

While talking with each woman, Trudy would get all riled up about what she heard and give her full-hearted support and comfort to each one. The next day, however, when Trudy saw Jan and Lucy laughing together on their lunch hour, and all but ignoring her, she realized she was being used; she was the "monkey in the middle."

Initially, you may be flattered to be everyone's confidant. However, eventually you'll only feel hurt and drained, particularly when you discover that these same people you've given your support to really don't have time to lend you support when you have problems of your own. Their only real use for you is when you're wholeheartedly mouthing what you know they want you to say.

The Hurt Of Being Seduced By The Cobra

Are you attracted to people who are subtly similar to the kind of people you have in your family? For example, at a party are you attracted to someone whom you later realized had reminded you of someone in your own family, or maybe someone you used to know? But this particular person seemed more comfortable to be with or even a little bit "better." Somehow this attraction feels more right than other attractions you have had. These enticing relationships usually start out cozy and comfortable, but later turn foul with horrors that are all too familiar. You find yourself hurt once again.

To prevent the hurt that comes with being attracted to people, especially if they have similarities to people in your family, go into new relationships slow and easy. Watch the signs along the way, so you won't be caught off guard or be taken for a fool. If a person seems too good to be true, especially if you have desperately wanted a relationship, your hunch could be right. If you feel almost too comfortable at the first meeting, you may think you have met your soul mate. However, keep in mind you could also be in the process of meeting an old issue in a new, more appealing costume.

Steps Toward Managing Your Hurt

Part of living is experiencing the honest feelings you have, and hurt is certainly one of them. If you devise a type of system for dealing with your hurt feelings and losses, you'll be able to get through the pain much easier. Otherwise, it will build up and later explode.

Support groups, therapy and talking to people close to you can be helpful. However, there may be times when friends and relatives can't give you the objectivity you may need to make up your own mind. Here are some steps to consider as you begin working towards managing your hurt feelings.

Eliminate The "How Could You Do This To Me" Attitude

When you think you know how someone will or should act on any given occasion, and the individual doesn't live up to your expectations, you're hurt and disappointed. You adopt a "How could you do this to me?" attitude.

Currently, you may realize life has too many dilemmas that invite you to wonder, "How could they do this to me?" or, Why is this happening to me? " If this is the case, you may want to seek outside input to help you gain insights as to what you may need to learn. If you continue to deny your past hurts, or stay in a victim-dependent role, you could remain forever in the crazy-making game of "How could you do this to me." "He did this to me again," or "This always happens to me," or "She hurts me every time I start to trust her again." Stop and think about what you're saying.

If this situation is still so intolerable, why are you still there? Or, why do you keep attracting these situations to you? Haven't you had enough? Perhaps, instead of focusing on the other person, consider what part you are playing that keeps it all going.

Don't Allow Others To Manipulate Your Life

Here's an example of how perceptions can create hurt feelings.

On the way to a game, Bob got into a minor "fender-bender" accident. In a hurry and was tailgating the car ahead. His friend George was in the car with him. When Bob went to get the car fixed, Bob insisted that George

pay half. George was shocked at Bob's request and explained that since he wasn't the driver he wasn't at fault and shouldn't pay. Bob responded by saying that he was rushing so they both could get to the football game oand he knew George to wanted get there on time.

While the argument continued, George felt like the life-long friendship was going downhill. George felt that Bob all too often had asked him to go above and beyond the call of duty. In turn, Bob expected George to help him with the situation because he had done so many times before.

George later admitted he remained friends with Bob because Bob had so few friends, and George's desire to be needed continued to keep him in the relationship. Both young men were hurt and angry. They weren't able to understand the needs and sensitivities of each other or themselves.

Although the interaction may seem petty, and you may agree with George's viewpoint more than Bob's, the fact remains that this type of scenario goes on in everyone's life. Marriages, in fact, often go the same route with arguments bordering on the ridiculous. Think about some of the half-witted disagreements you have had that got way out of hand.

Now, think about some of your everyday crazy-making problems with other people. Were you upset because of a one-time conflict? Or, after many of the same conflicts, did you find yourself in a pattern with this person where it always seems to go downhill the same way every time? Is it like a dance? You both know the routine, but neither of you is insightful enough to change the steps.

Think about approaching each interaction as though it were the first and only one with this person. In the above example, George could have said, "I never asked you to rush to the point of getting into an accident, and I wouldn't. I think each driver is responsible for his own driving. As much as I care about you, I can't comply with your request. If you need to be angry for awhile, I'll understand."

If a relationship means a lot to you, try getting your point across as calmly and logically as possible rather than getting into an emotional tirade about right and wrong. If the difference is petty, let it go as much as possible. (Also, so often, we feel required to get in a major huff over things as if our dignity depends on it. In reality, our getting upset and angry only serves to ensure that the other person misses our point completely and becomes more alienated from us.)

Alter Your Perspective Yet One More Time

Some people can forgive being lied to more easily than others. Others can get over the sting of infidelity, while some would rather die than forgive the other party. Our feelings about human transgressions usually go back to our childhood and we often relate to our parents' behavior patterns. It helps to look at your situation from as many points of view as you are able to.

❀ Is it possible you feel hurt because you think everyone is ganging up on you, when in reality they're not?

❀ Is there possibly a good explanation for the hurtful situation, if you give the other side a chance to explain?

❋ Is it possible the other person is really seeking your attention and love in a mishandled manner?

❋ Is it possible you set yourself up for this misunderstanding? Do you see a pattern of these misunderstandings throughout your life?

❋ Did you see yourself as a victim in this scenario from the beginning? Did you set this up in any way?

❋ Do you want to get over the hurt yet?

❋ Did this situation prompt you to take serious steps to make a change?

Whatever you do, the choice is yours. Many marriages can work through heartaches and lies, and many friendships can survive through jealousy and pride, as difficult as it may be at the time. Families have been able to get through issues regarding secrets and suicide. It's a matter of what *you* can endure and what *you* are willing to let go of.

If your ultimate goal is peace and healing you'll work through the process of pain, at your own pace, and eventually let go when you are ready because you will want to move away from the negative emotional baggage.

Sometimes, you may want to emotionally distance yourself from the relationship or situation for periods of time to take an emotional breather. This break also gives you a chance to alter your perspective and gain new insight. You may even decide to learn what you can and leave the situation entirely. Sometimes it's not healthy to hang in there. You may want to exit when the going gets too rough for you to survive in a healthy way. Again, the choice is yours.

Build Lines Of Communication

You may think there is no way to communicate with the other person. Or you may choose to be silent and act as though you are not hurt, even when everyone knows differently. Or, you may find that every time you do try to express yourself honestly, you or the other individual blows up.

Before giving up complete communication with the other person, first write all your thoughts on paper. Realistically determine how much you feel the "other side" could handle. Also, try to determine what is true about the other person, and what old perceptions you may have playing inside your own head.

Many times it's important to express the hurts you are harboring. As painful as it may be to fully experience memories and reminders of sadness and inequities, examining them can help you to get over them and stop you from continually going through similar situations.

Leaving The Situation

Over time you can decide if this is an environment or situation you want to stay in or leave, but you don't have to decide right away, unless you are in imminent danger. Consider Eli's case.

Eli belonged to a religious organization that required him to give up his individuality and to conform to the organization's standards and viewpoints. Eli found this hard to do. However, he tried every way he could to fit in and to please the pecking order. It seemed the harder he tried, the worse he was treated.

Somehow, it never occurred to him that this group might not be right for him and there were other religious and spiritual organizations in the world with more autonomous views and more loving attitudes, with a lot to offer. But he didn't seek out this type of group. He just stayed in this organization, hoping to please everybody and get them to treat him with the appreciation he wanted. It never happened.

Finally, Eli was thrown out. At first he thought it was the worst thing that could have ever happened. Later, however, as he made his way through a bumpy life, he found people and places that provided an atmosphere for peace and happiness. He even began to create his own satisfaction and enjoyment. Eventually, he began to understand how he had unconsciously reconstructed his own family dynamics in almost every situation he got into. The more he came to see how it happened, the better life got. Eli realized he had never acknowledged how frightening and demoralizing his relatives had been to him. As a child he remembered thinking his life depended on finding a way to get even the meanest people to take a liking to him. He wasn't able, especially as a child, which is understandable, to see that it wasn't his fault. Some of his family members truly were very unloving, self-centered people who were too busy reacting to their own problems to think about Eli's needs.

Over time, Eli came to find that his own parents were mistreated as children. They, in turn, passed the same treatment onto him; they knew no other way to raise a child.

Eli realized he needed to feel and grieve some painful feelings he had buried over time in order to move on. He also began to see how he had continued his old pattern of "trying to save the day," when, of course, he could not. The double binds he got entangled in were no-win situations.

Eventually, Eli would learn to spot potential heartaches sooner rather than later; he was able to determine if he should stay in an organization or a relationship as he gained more insight. During the times he decided to leave a dilemma, he learned to think ahead and pull out emotionally before he actually left physically.

If you choose to leave a situation, consider the following points:

❋ **Don't jump out of the pan into the fire.** When you are in a rough and painful dilemma, almost any situation will seem better than the one you are in. *Be careful.* Don't kid yourself. If you don't know what part you played in getting into your predicament, you may find yourself getting into the same type of problem again or maybe one that's worse. If you are presently in a harrowing or upsetting situation, go over the chattering monkeys exercise and study all your options. As bad as your experience may be at the moment, it could actually get worse instead of better. In fact, you could want to come back to the very situation you're now desiring to leave.

❃ **Get your ducks in a row first.** Often, just when you need clear thinking the most, your emotions kick in and you act ineffectively and unrealistically. If ultimately leaving the situation is your best option, it's important to lay the groundwork so that you land on your feet.

As an example, a spouse leaving an unhappy marriage may not fully look at all the financial considerations. "He can keep the house, and I don't care about spousal support. I just don't ever want to see him again," she says. Shortly down the road, however, she's so desperate for money and shelter, she decides to go back for one more round. (*If the situation with her husband is life threatening, then she should definitely not return. She could get help with friends, relatives or go to a shelter until she can create more viable options. Unfortunately, some people actually do return to life-threatening situations, sometimes as if their life depended on it!*)

The same scenario also holds true for people who immediately quit their jobs following a hurtful job review or an office misunderstanding. Unfortunately, they don't consider where they'll find their next job, or how they'll support themselves until then.

❃ **Always think through the ramifications of making dramatic changes in your life.** If you're sure that's what you want to do, make a game plan. You might even discuss your idea with a few friends or a counselor, attorney, financial specialist or career planner. Don't let poor planning keep you from succeeding in your attempt to improve your life.

❃ **Cross your bridges, don't burn them.** If you find yourself getting involved in emotional problems with friends, family or co-workers, take care not to let your hurt feelings compromise your reasoning. You could end up destroying all your bridges and having to start all over again. There may be times when people truly disappoint you, but that doesn't mean you have to turn them into enemies. The situation is probably difficult enough as it is.

Practice Forgiveness

You may want to read *The Practice Of Forgiveness—Transforming An Enemy Into A Friend* by Linda Bates. It's an excellent book for helping you alter your perspective about forgiveness. It also serves as a lifesaver for those times when you feel you've tried everything, and you still can't get over the hurt.

Forgiveness and letting go of hurt doesn't mean that you have to minimize what has gone on. Rather, it involves a conscious decision on your part to recognize that the other person will only change by maturing on his or her own or by getting help. Also, the person may have been dealing with his own issues and did not mean to hurt you. It helps to remember the following: On the pathway to forgiveness, *you* are the only person you can change, not someone else.

Final Resolve

Hurt is finally resolved when you come to the realization that you no longer ache about something you thought you would never get over. Whether it be a change in perception, interacting with others to bring about positive change, or leaving the situation, true resolution to life's hurts comes when you let go of the sting of the dilemma or the power it had over you.

Consider how difficult it must have been for these people to manage their hurt:

❈ *After two years, Sheila was finally getting on with life by forgiving her husband who had accidentally run over and killed their 15-month old daughter as he was backing the car out of the driveway.* (This is perhaps one of the most difficult situations to overcome. Losing a child is considered to be a catastrophe beyond most serious events. Also, the fact that Sheila was so upset with her husband, understandably so, prevented them from sharing their grief as a couple.)

❈ *Bill is getting over the hurt of his wife's affair with a co-worker. He realizes that he wants to stay with Mary and work things out more than he wants to stay hurt about the fling she had at a corporate convention. The fact that Mary also wants the relationship to succeed is helping Bill to heal.*

❈ *Anne at 49-years-old, comes to the realization that the hurt she felt she received from her mother comes from her mother's own fear, jealousy, and intimidation more than an intent to hurt her daughter. When Anne lets go of the old hurts and realizes that her mother will not change, she is able to recognize, acknowledge and accept the love her mother also offers.*

❈ *Al finally left his job after three years because he was always feeling unappreciated and had experienced a lot of grief and aggravation as well. Before he left however, he took a few computer courses at night so he was fully prepared to make the move. After settling into his new position, he wished he had left the job sooner, but he understood the necessity of having a paycheck while he prepared himself for a new career.*

❋ *Gwen finally speaks up and tells her husband that she can barely stand to be around him. She withheld her feelings until he had recovered from a near fatal car accident caused by his angry refusal to let another car pass him on the highway. His long silences and dark moods—coping methods he used as a youngster to deal with his deep depressions and dark side—have upset her. Much to her surprise, he listened for the first time and sought help from a therapist. However, if he hadn't, she was financially and emotionally prepared to leave. She had talked about allthis before in vain but now, her husband took her seriously because he realized that she had options and wasn't completely dependent on him. Also, he finally realized the seriousness of his self-sabotaging behavior and saw how it could cause his own death.*

Resolve. It's one of those wonderful times when you either look at life in an entirely new way, or when you become proactive doing what you need to do to free yourself from feeling victimized or hurt. You learn to work through the pain, clearing the way for happiness to enter your life.

One thing is certain; when you're brave enough to see through life's hurts and forego the "eye for an eye" mentality, your chances of resolving your pain increase many times over. So does your joy.

8

YOU DON'T HAVE TO DO GREAT THINGS TO DESERVE LOVE!

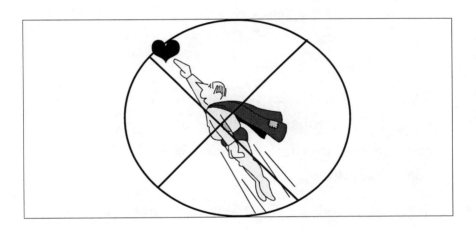

Think about all your achievements for a minute. Have you spent your entire life believing you have to do something remarkable to gain attention or love? Are your expectations for your life or career so high, you often become frustrated and overwhelmed? Do you push yourself in the quest for success to the point of burning out? Or, do you ever feel you'll never live up to your own or someone else's expectations so you feel it's not worth trying?

A Game of "Can You Top This?"

Here's a story of what one woman went through to gain recognition and love from her family. With all her efforts she never achieved what she wanted. This example may bring memories of the various extremes you too have gone through simply for a few moments of attention from your family, friends or co-workers.

The incident for Ellen occurred at a family barbecue hosted by her best-intentioned grandmother. For years, Ellen's family get-togethers had been battlefields of rivalry for Ellen, her sister Gwen and her cousin Paul, while the senior members of the family looked on.

During this particular version of "Dazzle the Family" game, Paul was in limbo with nothing much to report. Gwen had been going through some rough times so she was down a notch. Not Ellen, however. She was racing full speed ahead.

Wearing a flashy black and yellow, size-six dress, Ellen took center stage, cackling away about her two-year contract with a consulting group. Uncle Charles oohing and ahhing while Ellen showed off her expensive 4-color presentation folder, said, "Ellen, you are really in a position to make something of yourself here."

Frenetically moving around the room, Ellen relished her spotlight role in gaining the family's momentary attention with her recent accomplishment. Meanwhile, Gwen and Paul sat silently as Ellen blabbed away. During and after her performance, Paul never looked at her, and neither he nor Gwen offered their congratulations. And why should they? This threesome had been playing the "can you top this" game for years within the nuclear and extended family.

Shortly after achieving her few minutes of attention, Ellen and Gwen got ready to go play a game of tennis. While they were all walking toward the court, within earshot she heard her father tell Gwen, "I'll give you five bucks if you beat the hell out of her."

Months later, after Ellen had gone through an auto accident, a near divorce, and a bout of major depression, she realized her frantic moves to put her own dent in the planet were, in fact, ruining her life.

Isn't it amazing what you will go through just to gain a couple of minutes of attention or a few words of recognition? Perhaps you can relate to this saga of always struggling to outdo yourself. Maybe you, too, place demands on yourself that can put you over the edge.

Are You Caught In The "Can You Top This" Game?

If you associate your work, accomplishments and productivity with deserving love and acceptance, you may end up losing the people you truly care about. By the time you realize all your eggs are in the "outer world" basket, your family and friends may be pursuing their lives without you. You may also not appreciate those who do love and accept you just the way you are.

If you are uncertain whether you fall into the category of seeking love and acceptance mainly through work and productivity, ask yourself the following questions:

1. Do you constantly feel driven to throw yourself into a work-related activity?

2. Do you work on weekends or even take work with you on vacations, giving you have less time for relaxation with your significant other or your family?

3. Do you feel guilty if you let a day go by without working on a project?

4. Do you sometimes feel your family doesn't show enough pride in your accomplishments?

5. Do you often chase your family away when you are concentrating on a work-related project at home?

6. Is it difficult for you to fully enjoy a quiet moment or a beautiful sunset unless you have recently finished a major accomplishment or met a particular deadline?

7. Are you envious of people who seem more accomplished or famous than you?

8. Do you fantasize that when you become rich and famous your parents and siblings will finally give you the attention and recognition you deserve?

If you answered yes on two or more of these questions, you may be over-compensating, to some degree, to make yourself more worthy of love and attention.

Ways To Put Your Life And Achievements Into Perspective

If you find yourself having to continually produce or to work to gain love and acceptance, here are a few suggestions to help you put your life into perspective.

Acknowledge Something About Yourself That Is Good Or Worthwhile Right Now

Describe yourself in the most realistically positive light that you can at this time.

* ❋ What are you doing well?

* ❋ What do you have a good chance of accomplishing that you have set out to do?

* ❋ What do you love and except about yourself even when you know you are far from perfect? (We're all far from "perfect.")

* ❋ Even if you feel you are not living up to your own expectation or the projected expectations of your parents or others, what is something you can say that you appreciate about yourself?

Whatever your answers, take time to acknowledge the good within. If your job or an activity has different levels of attainment, choose a comfortable level of involvement that won't set you up for frustration and possible failure. Make a conscious effort to enjoy each plateau of progress without always thinking you have to immediately outdo your last accomplishment.

Take pride in what you are doing right now. Do not belittle

your present task, or career or yourself. Don't get stuck thinking that you can't do anything, work or play, unless it is unusually productive or extremely rewarding financially. (There are people who will not get out of bed unless they have a job that rivals the President's! For them it's all or nothing.)

Create A Space For Your Happiness Now— Don't Wait

Right now, acknowledge and accept some portion of yourself as being worthy of your happiness. It's often said that success is getting what you want and happiness is wanting what you get. If you don't create your own happiness now, you will only appreciate your accomplishments for a short while before you find a new mountain to climb to prove you are acceptable and lovable again. Thus, you will always be frustrated.

Most importantly, refrain from making the statement, "I'll be happy when I finally do this" or "I'll feel good about myself when I finally accomplish that." This type of thinking sabotages any pleasure you get in the process. It can become so debilitating, you may never finish what you started out to do. You become frozen in fear of failure and project disappointment that things won't turn out the way you wanted.

Take care not to attach your major accomplishments or over-achieving goals to who you ARE, thinking that you are only as good as your last act. If you continually feel you haven't produced enough, or if you only feel "alive" when you're doing something "big," you will tear down the very essence of your being. You won't appreciate the people and situations that truly mean the most to you—your children, spouse, friends, colleagues and so on. Even quiet, peaceful moments will elude you. And frankly, those moments are some of our most important times. There is a sense of overwhelming peace when a person realizes the greatest achievement is to be able to live in the moment and feel all is well within. Examples of this can be when you can sit and hold your child and stroke her hair or watch your pet rabbit eat, or see a beautiful sunset which feels like the grandest moment you can remember.

Consider your many qualities. Don't judge whether or not they are important. Write them down; see the value in each one.

Define and claim your own happiness. Accepting ourselves the way we are and honoring our own happiness are more important than anything else we could possibly do. It's more important to be truly ourselves than it is to be "important" only for the purpose of gaining the attention of others.

Plan A Day With Loved Ones

Set aside some time or a special day to be with family or people you care about, when you can give them all of your attention. You may want to spend time with these people in a group or be with them individually.

Make a point of creating memories for yourself and for your loved ones. Work on disciplining yourself to focus on the love and intimacy of the situation. If you begin feeling torn by your need to get back to work, put these work thoughts on hold, and focus on simply feeling the importance of the moment. You can always return to your work when your loved ones are busy and unavailable to you. If you want, you can even pick an actual time and date when you will return to your work so you will feel you have "control" over your time and how it is spent.

Remember, you can't do days over again, and the ones that really count are in your heart, not in your head. Take pictures to remember those times. Your activities don't need to be extraordinary to deserve pictures. It's the simple moments that are special.

Take Time To Bask In Everything You Have Accomplished

You may want to develop a profile of all your accomplishments. Recognize that the more you accept yourself for who you are, the less you will need to look at this list or your resume to feel valid. None the less, as you accomplish your goals and pursuits, add them to your list. Truly *enjoy* each of your accomplishments. Savor each activity you complete. Keep a scrapbook of business cards and letters from people who have appreciated you in some way. Separate these accomplishments from your personal life. Realize that even without all of these accolades you are going through life with some grace, and you are worthwhile for just getting this far.

Use Social Activity As A Service And Benefit

Do you find you only feel "worthy" when you are getting attention from others? Then you may find yourself feeling like you are "disappearing" when you are in a group of people and don't stand out in some way. You may not understand why you feel this way or that you are even doing it.

In work-related groups or social clubs, make a point of getting involved for the benefit of others as well as for yourself. Approach work or social organizations as if it's a privilege for you to serve others. Feel free to give what you can and "sing your heart out." If you make room for others in the group to benefit along with you, you will be better received and appreciated for your efforts. If you really are doing some "big" things, involving others and helping them, as well as letting them help you, this truly makes you a wonderful person. Also, you will probably evoke less jealousy from people when you don't come from the standpoint of just aggrandizing yourself.

When you do stand out and become a "star," play your part, then blend in again. Consider it a privilege to play a leadership role, but know there's also plenty to gain from sitting back and letting others shine when it's their turn. You get a better grasp of the big picture and a better sense of yourself when you are part of the crowd and don't take yourself so seriously.

Recognize That Your Life Is Your Career

If making money is your only means of pumping up your self-esteem, there's a good chance you are not getting your money's worth! Begin looking at your entire life as your career. Daily, acknowledge yourself as a total person. Project your self-esteem away from the job. Fill in the blanks with self-appreciation, good relationships and fun activities that make you a more well-rounded person.

Don't judge yourself on what you do from Monday through Friday alone. While work is certainly an important component to a fulfilled life, you are missing the point if that is all you focus on. Schedule fun time, prayer, and/or meditation as if it were a business meeting. Throw yourself into it as though it's something you absolutely must do and create a deadline to get it done.

Create A Less Frenetic Pace

The book, *Slowing Down in a Speeded Up World,* by Adair Lara, is helpful in understanding that "little things" are really the big moments. Learn to live your life in a way that makes you want to look forward to each day. There is no gold star at the end of the road if you busy yourself each day to the point of collapsing in the hope of being discovered and appreciated in a way that may not be at all realistic. Susan Ertz, quoted in the above-mentioned book, states it well—"Millions of persons long for immortality who do not know what to do with themselves on a rainy afternoon."

Know When To Say No

Try saying no to a project or offer you would consider doing only out of fear of rejection or alienation. Sometimes saying no to others is saying yes to yourself. The words yes and no are more important than many people realize. Saying these words, and we say them often, continually shapes our lives much like the tools we use to make pottery or to sculpt a form. The more you can be clear about what to say yes to and what to say no to, the more you will experience inner and outer harmony. When you go along with the program and say yes to someone, hoping you can duck out at a later date, you are not living a proactive and productive life, and you are not in harmony with life's bigger picture.

Don't Compare Yourself To Others

Make a list of five acquaintances or idols you feel are successful in some way. Write down how and why they are so accomplished. Then consider their burdens and flaws if you know them. They all have hurdles, possibly ones you would never want to have to overcome yourself. As much as you might fantasize about being someone else, his or her life can't really be more right for you than your own. The sooner you let go of envying or idolizing others and focus on your own assets and challenges, the better off you will be. Learn from them as much as you can, but focus on your own special uniqueness.

Don't Put All Your Ambition Eggs Into One Basket

One of the surest ways to meet with disappointment is to decide that there is only one avenue available for your success, and if you don't take that particular avenue you will be a complete failure.

One young man went to medical school to become a neurosurgeon. Although he became a competent surgeon in training, he couldn't pass his boards after five attempts. He then drowned his sorrows in alcohol and ended up in the psychiatric ward of a nearby hospital. After much help, he later taught at a medical school and did quite well. His adjustment was admirable because he eventually was able to help others with similar experiences.

Many career tracks appear all consuming—pro football, dancing, acting, law school, or dental school, for example. It's necessary to be focused, committed and motivated to achieve your career dream. However, it's important to consider the big picture and to remain flexible so you can make directional changes if you come to a dead end. Throw yourself wholeheartedly into a project or career direction, but always have a contingency plan in case events don't turn out the way you planned.

An Olympic ice skater once said, "Well, there's always Medical school," after not winning the gold metal on one particular occasion. This person had a contingency plan!

An excellent book, *Handbook to Higher Consciousness*, by Ken Keyes, Jr., stresses the importance of making your life a "parade of preferences." This parade keeps you from getting overly attached to any single aspect of life as a requirement for your happiness.

Enjoy The Process Of Your Endeavors

Recognize that the *process* is actually more important than the *outcome*. It may take fortitude to look at life like this; however, if you begin to see value in all parts of a process, you will be able to truly live in the moment. You will feel less compelled to rush to the finish line and begin your search for another race. Choose your life tasks as if each day would be an end in itself. In reality, life could end at any moment, and it's our moments that make our lives.

Accept Love Unconditionally

If you have spent your life believing you must do something remarkable to gain love from those around you, you may have difficulty accepting that you can be loved for just being yourself. If someone is attentive or loving, you may immediately become suspicious. The story of Maria is a perfect example of this type of thinking.

During the early years of Maria's marriage, she acted as though she was too creative and mentally advanced for her husband. In fact, she left him for a while because she was certain he was holding her back from doing great and wonderful things. Looking back, Maria finally understood that deep down she didn't feel she deserved his love because she couldn't accept herself. Her husband wasn't holding her back from anything.

Thanks to his willingness to hang in there, Maria eventually re-entered their marriage. Slowly, she learned to trust him. She realized that a trap door wasn't going to open up and drop her in a hole where she would be by herself. She has learned now that she deserves the love people are willing to give her. She has come to love herself without conditions.

We each have a vision of "unconditional love." It could be defined as love with no strings attached. You simply feel a deep compelling sense of love and compassion for someone. Your feelings don't depend on the other person's strengths, faults or opinion of you. But having unconditional love for someone doesn't mean you accept abuse from the person or agree with all her actions.

Steps To Learn To Accept Unconditional Love

It's wonderful to love yourself unconditionally. It doesn't mean you're conceited, just self-appreciating and forgiving. Here are some steps to consider in learning to accept love unconditionally:

1. List all the people who are loving and kind to you. It might be helpful to go through the alphabet from A to Z and think of those you love. Take a few minutes and bask in the feeling that you are loved. Envision how you want these relationships to go. You don't necessarily have to be with these people every day, but knowing they support you is important.

2. Think about the positive words and smiles you have received from people over the past week. You may want to write down their words or picture them repeating kind remarks to you.

3. Save uplifting letters and notes you have received. Read them from time to time to be reminded of your worthiness.

4. Place photos of people who love you in your bedroom. Remind yourself of their love for you, your love for them and your love for yourself. Collages and scrapbooks also work. Let your surroundings mirror love and acceptance.

5. Write a letter to yourself or make an audio tape explaining why you deserve success and happiness right now. It may sound awkward telling yourself how wonderful you are, but realize this exercise isn't to boost your ego. It is a genuine and innocent step towards appreciating and understanding yourself just as you are.

6. Make time every day to tell yourself that you are worthy of unconditional love. Do this exercise for 10-15 minutes every day at the same time, perhaps before you go to bed or when you wake up. When you allow yourself to sit still for any length of time, you are validating your sense of being. Few things are as important as learning to accept yourself. Breathe deeply during this exercise. Deep breaths are signs that you feel deserving of what the universe has to offer you. Take note of times when it is difficult to take a deep breath. This may indicate that you are upset or insecure about something that needs to be faced.

7. Practice being honest with others and, as I've discussed before, say no to requests that you are unable to fulfill or handle. It's often difficult to say no or to tell others your honest feelings, particularly if you are afraid they will no longer accept you if you present yourself in a different manner from what they have come to expect. At the very least, by saying no, you will find out if others are accepting or loving you unconditionally. At the very most, your honesty and authenticity will demonstrate how much you really do love and accept yourself just the way you are.

8. Condition yourself to stop at least once day and look around you to capture and to savor a moment, especially when you feel unconditionally acceptable (even very happy). These moments may not come naturally in the beginning; it may take practice. As you program yourself to do this, you will

find, even on the days when everything goes wrong, you will be able to savor a special moment.

Over time, you can even come to savor moments that are not particularly fun or easy but help you gain insight and view life from a new perspective. This will contribute immensely to your growth and help you gain more compassion for yourself and others.

9

MOVING ON WITH LIFE
TWO STEPS
FORWARD,
ONE STEP BACK

An oft quoted phrase is "All things come in three's," good or bad. However, when life starts going downhill, it doesn't necessarily happen in three's. Problems often seem to multiply, taking on a momentum of their own. They can crash upon you as though floodgates suddenly opened and everything bad came rushing through. Of course, this isn't necessarily the reality of what's actually happening, but it may often seem that way.

After it's over, there are moments when positive things begin to emerge. You feel better, more relaxed. You realize you've lived through something you thought would push you over the edge, but it didn't. Even if it did, and you survived, you can realize that often people require being in the most extreme straits to shock them back into the true spirit of life.

This is the amazing phenomena of life—you overcome dilemmas all the time, even if you don't fully realize it. People overcome the fear of living alone; others deal with bankruptcy; some cope with a move from a place of familiarity to the unknown.

Whether it's from the help of angels or just good luck, some semblance of order usually takes control during difficult periods, often just when you're sure you can't take any more. Here are several examples of people who got through everyday crazy making and survived.

Marilyn was alone one night in her "safe" home when she saw someone shine a flashlight through one of the windows in her apartment. She saw the light follow her as she ran from room to room trying to escape the light. She was petrified and panicked. Her screams awakened a neighbor who called the police. Fortunately, the police got there in the nick of time, just as the burglar was breaking in.

After falling apart from this terrifying experience, Marilyn pulled herself together and took positive action. She moved to a another place with roommates, and with help, worked through her trauma until she could let it go. Now, she looks back in awe that she got through the experience fairly well.

Bill was madly in love with his girlfriend when she suddenly broke up with him. He was devastated and sure he would never get over the heartbreak. Months went by. Suddenly, one day he woke up and discovered that his heart wasn't beating fast with the pain anymore. He took a deep breath and realized that he was no longer grieving. In fact, he realized his life was actually better without her; he no longer had to suffer through her moodiness and sharp criticism.

Sherry came close to losing her daughter in a dreadful accident. She spent days agonizing while her daughter was in intensive care. It took every ounce of strength not to succumb to feelings of desperation. Eventually, her daughter survived. Although she wept with joy, it was months before she could stop worrying that her daughter might be in another accident. Months later, she realized that her worry had mostly subsided.

Jim came home from his wife's annual Christmas party upset and disturbed. During a conversation with Greg, one of the attorneys in his wife's office, Jim discovered that prior to meeting him, his wife Lili had had a longstanding intimate relationship with Greg, a co-worker who is still her good friend.

His wife had never mentioned her earlier attraction to Greg, and worse yet, a number of people Jim spoke to at the party seemed to know all the details of one of their recent fights. This information troubled Jim to the point of negatively affecting his relationship with his wife. Finally, he came to grips with his issue, and now with the passing of time, Jim wonders why he made such a "big deal" out of the situation.

Laurie had just gotten a divorce, and the child custody battle was worse than she ever imagined. Her ex-husband had fought a dirty fight, and she became physically ill every time she thought about the scenes in court. In fact, her illnesses became so intense, she began missing days at work. One day, after receiving help from a therapist, Laurie realized that she was making herself sick over both the divorce and past events in her life. She made a decision to call and invite her ex-husband to pick up and enjoy his children the next weekend. From then on, Laurie was able to adjust and to regain her health. Although Laurie never did like her ex-husband, the idea of custody battles lost its power to make her ill.

These are the types of experiences that are devastating when you go through them, but later you look back and marvel that you made it. However, if you're going through a life-shattering dilemma now, you may be questioning whether or not you have what it takes to get through this one, too. Even if things are slowly getting better, you may wonder if a trap door will open any moment to drop you to a more terrifying place.

If you're in the process of mending right now, tell yourself that life is ever-changing and you can deal with whatever comes up, even if it's feeling just plain chaotic. You know you can get through this because you have made it through tough times before. When life is rocky and chaotic, look to your strengths. Know that tomorrow will be better. You may even start to welcome the changes.

If you feel you have little strength to hold you up, you may want to ask your "Higher Self" or "Supreme Being" to help you. You may need to pray or meditate. Whatever methods might have helped in the past, use them now. A passage from *God Calling God at Eventide* offers reassurance for many people from all walks of life:

"It is not passionate appeal that gains the Divine Ear so much as the quiet placing of the difficulty and worry in the Divine Hands. So trust and be no more afraid than a child would be, who places its tangled skein of wool in the hands of a loving mother and runs out to play, pleasing the mother more by its unquestioning confidence than if it went down on its knees and implored her help, which would pain her the rather, as it would imply she was not eager to help when help was needed."

Many people strongly believe that the universe operates by moving in the direction of what you completely and positively focus on, and if you do this without worry or fear it is enough to pull you through. A particular religious affiliation may not be necessary for you. It is only suggested here that each individual make peace within himself in a manner most comfortable to him.

Setbacks Do Not Ruin The Progress You Have Made

There's an important lesson to be learned when the Winter Olympics roll around. Watch the figure skaters with their grace and poise. Also watch when one of them falls... she simply picks herself up and continues her routine. She doesn't even brush herself off. Instead, she continues where she left off with a beautiful smile, despite the fact she is devastated. She knows that the fall costs points, but she also realizes the importance of recouping and regaining her composure to continue with the routine. (It would serve no purpose to collapse and let her emotions out, although she may do this later in private.)

Consider the following points:

❋ It's possible to feel that one setback can demolish all the progress you have made. This just isn't true. All good things take time, just remember life is a parade of experiences and lessons to be learned. (Some lessons just have a higher price tag than others.) Learn to stand back and observe your behavior and other's without judgment. Keep learning from yourself and others how to keep crazy making out of your life.

❋ Let yourself off the hook; you don't have to ruminate over every less-than-perfect situation, ripping into yourself with "should have's." When you are all tied up about mistakes you've made, you won't be able to fully consider all the options you have in front of you right now, or all the valuable insights you might gain.

❋ Sometimes our setbacks result from not using good judgment. Perhaps you made a certain decision based on someone else's advice and not your own gut feeling. Most of us do have good judgment. We need to learn to trust our own feelings more.

Don't ever believe that others have a given right to make mistakes and you don't. Each of us has difficult areas, and we get seduced into going back and making mistakes again and again. It's far better to contemplate your Achilles' Heel than it is to beat yourself up about it. Make friends with your perceived flaws. These are simply your lessons in life.

Dealing With Critical People And Making Your Own Decisions

Life is filled with hurdles. One of your hurdles may be learning how to deal with people who are overly critical of you or who make tactless remarks to you, even when the comments come under the guise of "I only want what's best for you." Another challenge may be learning when to make your own decisions and when to consider other people's advice.

Don't fall into the trap of being a whipping boy or letting other people's comments devastate you. Learn to hold your own by listening to your own true, inner thoughts. Although you, like everyone else, may occasionally need helpful input from others, be careful who you turn to. You don't want people with problems of their own to use your problems to make themselves feel better by subtly putting you down.

Steve is an example of someone who needed some helpful advice. Because his parents always put down his ideas, he came to believe his own thoughts were not worthwhile.

Steve was never able to keep a job or to save money. His in-laws gave him start-up money for several businesses, but they all failed. Money always seemed to slip through his hands. Steve's financial problems destroyed his marriage. His wife left him after he almost ruined her credit.

When his wife left, Steve began working with a high-roller investor, who made him feel like a hot-shot high risk taker in the market. This investor led him down the wrong path. Again, Steve was stuck with bills and liability.

Eventually, he sought the help of a financial planner, who calmly and plainly, without judging or criticizing Steve, showed him how his lifestyle and spending habits were setting him up for failure. Steve listened. Because he did listen and follow the advice, Steve was able to alter the course of his life. The financial planner first showed Steve that he cared about him. Then, Steve trusted him enough to listen.

The lesson is to take advice from someone who is honest with you and may at times confront your with realities that may be difficult to hear. However, it's best if it is someone who doesn't tear you down or flatter you to boost your ego. Think about the motto I once read on a hospital wall: "People don't care how much you know until they know how much you care."

When To Listen To Yourself

Although Steve, in the above example, learned to listen to others who were helpful and to follow through himself, ultimately we all have to make our own decisions. Even if you let someone else run your life, when all is said and done, there's no one to blame for your mistakes but you. It's also a waste of time to blame yourself or others. There are only lessons to learn and situations to experience.

Consider these points before you act on the advice of others:

1. Have you heard the same or similar comments before?

2. Does the advice empower you, or is it spillage from someone else's disappointments?

3. Does this person help you gain a new, more mature perspective, or do you find your world is even smaller and more negative when you listen to her?

4. Does this person have any redeeming qualities that make it truly worthwhile to spend time with her, or do you find yourself too often bothered by her presence?

5. Does this person seduce you into thinking her advice is what you want because you are desperate and will do anything he says? Or, do you feel a sense of peace that her advice is moving you in your most true and authentic direction?

Let your answers help you determine if the help from others is productive.

Crazy making often takes hold when you've been in a lifelong limbo of wondering what you want out of life, who you are, and where to go from here. If you don't know what you want, then how will you ever know if you're heading in the right direction? Also, while you are asking yourself questions about other people, ask yourself what you are all about.

Consider The Rest Of Your Life

Chapter 3 discussed planning the rest of your life by looking back at your life from the viewpoint of your old age. The following exercises are designed for that purpose. In order to complete these exercises, you will want a pencil and several sheets of paper.

NEWSPAPER ARTICLE EXERCISE

Although, it's been said "Life is what happens when you are making other plans," it's still helpful to at least have a picture of how you would like your life to go. You can take some unexpected journeys, but in the long run, there does appear a path you've followed, perhaps directed by your inner guides. To make use of the adage "Hindsight is 20/20," it can be helpful to look back at your life from a future viewpoint. Now, when you come to forks in the road, think carefully about how certain paths will possibly affect the ultimate outcome you had envisioned.

Pretend you are now at the end of your life and a major newspaper wants to write an article about who you are and what you've done. Ask yourself these questions:

❋ What are your proudest accomplishments?

❋ Did you pass up any opportunities? If so, why?

❋ Did you have a happy life?

❋ Did you have any regrets? What did you learn from them?

❋ What were the happy moments and what were the sad moments?

❋ What did other people say about you?

❋ How did you feel basically feel about yourself at any given moment, whether you were doing anything or not?

❋ What do you want to say about yourself?

As you go through the answers to these questions, remember you are working backwards. You still have the chance to alter your path in life *and* the feelings you have about yourself and others.

PLANNING THE REST OF YOUR LIFE EXERCISE

The next exercise is an opportunity to further consider where you'd like to focus your energy. It isn't always clear what steps to take in our lives. Hopefully this exercise will help you. It is divided into nine categories: goals; dreams; fantasies; challenges; things to cherish; situations to stay away from; regrets to work through, compromises to make, people to forgive; possible changes to make; and your legacy.

Goals

Many people have their goals in mind, but they don't make plans to achieve them. Others have such unrealistic goals, they set themselves up for disappointment when they can't achieve them.

These three important points can help you set your goals:

1. To help your mind hone in on a workable plan, understand that a realistic goal should be something that you have at least an 85 percent chance of accomplishing.

2. A goal should be something that is truly meaningful to you, not something your parents want you to accomplish or something that puts you in someone else's good graces.

3. A goal is something you make plans to achieve, and if one plan doesn't work, you try a contingency plan to achieve it.

A goal is different from a wish, which is to desire something that is out of your hands or the reach of your own efforts. Generally speaking, a wish is the hope that something will happen to save you from your present reality. It's fine to have wishes, as long as you understand that with goals, as opposed to wishes, you can take real direct steps to achieve them.

Write down your goals. While being as realistic as possible, extend your thoughts as far as you can take them so as not to sell yourself short. End up moving in a direction that is in line with your true interests and talents.

Dreams

Dreams are important. Different from wishes, dreams can be empowering if they flow from your heart and soul and make you feel inspired to do something because you were created to do it.

Here are a few points to consider about dreams:

❋ A dream is something you have a 5-20 percent chance of making happen. If you recognize the opportunity, you'll take it; if it doesn't happen, you can live without it, too.

❋ A goal can be a spin-off of a dream. For example, you dream about writing a book, then you actually write the book. Or, you dream of having your own talk show as a spin-off of your inspirational workshops, and it becomes a reality.

❋ You may dream of being calm most of the time. If that's your dream, you can move it closer to your goal by first practicing short periods of calmness and then progressing to longer periods. Actual implementation of any dream can help turn it into a goal.

❋ Enjoy the process of having your dreams. If you think you'll never be happy until you achieve all your dreams, you'll go through life an unhappy person. Happiness is enjoying the process along the way, not the end of the journey. Dreams are great opportunities to experience something in your soul before they come to fruition.

❋ Dreams are important and personal. Make sure you share them only with people who are supportive and non-judgmental. Write down your deepest inner dreams. Picture yourself in them, then picture them turning out just the way you want them in your mind. Explore how you feel every inch of the way.

Fantasies

When exciting, romantic and stimulating things occur more in your mind than in your real life, fantasies are born. Fantasies often do not become realities, and most of the time they are best left as fantasies. Fantasies are fun; all you need is your imagination. Take your fantasies and use them for inspiration when your life is in a rut. Enjoy them to the fullest, and don't limit yourself. But be in touch with reality at the same time. Don't let unreal fantasies take over your life. Differentiate between fun fantasies and your goals.

Sometimes it is fun to privately write down your fantasies to see if that is what they really are or if they are an extension of your dreams or even your goals.

Challenges

Challenges can be considered goals with a twist. Goals involve planning, usually within a time frame, while challenges are goals without a committed plan of action yet. For example, you may be thinking about losing 20 pounds, running the Boston marathon, giving up smoking, having lyposuction on your thighs, or forgiving old Aunt Ida for hurting your feelings, but you haven't done anything about it yet.

A challenge is between you and yourself. It's up to you to determine whether or not to move it to a goal. Remember, a goal is something you have an 85 percent or more chance of accomplishing.

Think about some activities or abilities, both physical and emotional, that you would like to accomplish. Write them down as challenges. Look at them carefully and decide if you have the ability, tenacity and opportunity to accomplish them as goals.

Things, Ideas, People And Places To Cherish

Happiness, appreciation of self and others, and pure joy are aspects that make life worth living. In fact, they may be the key to understanding what is meaningful in your daily existence. Things you can cherish are thoughts, statements, and pictures in your mind that you can access when times are rough. People, pets, places, concepts and ideas you believe to be true could also be cherished for the joy they bring into your life.

The more memories, feelings and moments or heartfelt love you have to cherish, the easier it will be to gather hope on a day when you especially need it. If you were falling in an airplane about to crash and you flashed your most joyous thoughts and moments in your mind, what would they be?

Write down the things you cherish. Be as spontaneous as possible. Try to allow yourself to consider those pictures that come to your mind freely. Don't determine what you should or should not be thinking.

Situations To Stay Away From

Throughout life you'll find things, people, places and activities you would do better to avoid. Sometimes, however, these are the very things we are drawn towards. Wild horses can hardly keep us away. Here are questions to ask yourself in deciding whether or not to add someone or something to your "stay away from" list:

❋ Do you have mixed feelings about this person, place or thing? Do you feel guilty or bad regarding your involvement?

❋ Does it occur to you that if you engage in a particular situation you are adding danger to your life and perhaps the lives of others in some way?

❋ If you spend time thinking about the situation, are you more confused than ever?

❋ Are you able to talk openly about the situation with most people, or is it something you can only discuss with people who go along with you?

❋ Do you find yourself making excuses about the situation?

The more uncomfortable the circumstance becomes at any given time, the more crazy making you are inviting into your life.

Write down any situations you know you should stay away from. You also might want to write why it's a good idea to avoid this situation. Describe why you are drawn to it and what will be the reward if you stay away. If you make up your mind to stay away, do you have a plan of action?

Regrets To Work Through, Compromises To Make, People To Forgive

The word "regret" often falls on deaf ears. You may be someone who rationalizes everything you have experienced in your life, and you may say it was well worth it; or you may be someone who can admit that you already paid too high a price for lessons you may not have yet learned. As you look back on your life, here are a few possible areas of regret: letting opportunities get away because of the needs of someone else; being sexually promiscuous; getting into a long-term relationship with the wrong person for you; letting your health go; taking a job to please someone else; and condemning people for things that you do or have done yourself.

Forgiveness is releasing burdensome thoughts—hate, anger, revenge, hurt—towards someone whom you feel has harmed you or others intentionally or unintentionally. Part of the process of forgiveness is grieving, not minimizing what happened. Forgiveness is part of your own healing process. Honor this process and don't let anyone rush you on until you're ready. Although you may think forgiveness is for the benefit of others, it's really for you.

Probably the greatest task in life, and one of your greatest opportunities, is to look in the mirror and accept yourself for who and what you are right now. Once you heal your own hurts and regrets, the more compassion you will have for others.

Write down regrets you have to work through, compromises you need to make, and people you want to forgive. It especially helps if you are not judgmental, critical or blame yourself or others when completing this part of the exercise.

Possible Changes To Make

As this book comes to a conclusion, consider other changes you may want to make in your life. For example, you may be working with a "real jerk," someone you deem unworthy of your respect.

Before writing the person off or leaving the job in a huff, think of how you can deal with the dilemma in ways that will help you learn more about yourself as well as the other person, ways that you might not have normally considered. The chances are high that you'll run into a similar dilemma down the line if you don't take this opportunity to learn what the situation says about you now.

Write down any changes you want to make.

Your Legacy

Last but not least, what are your greatest gifts to yourself, others and the universe? All your gifts are important.

The more use you make of your gifts, the greater your legacy and the more you make of your life. (If you can love yourself and others without judging them, that in itself is a great gift.)

Do you have great laughter, great love, joy, inner peace to offer? Can you write, speak, teach, care, listen, follow directions or lead? Whatever your gifts, write them down. Don't judge whether these gifts are "worthy" or "important."

Today Is A Gift

Whatever happens, your life is your creation and so are you. Be aware of when you are happy and when you are sad. Recognize the time to help others and when it is time to get help yourself.

For those times when life gets too crazy, hang on and know that you have an inner resource and reserve that can be activated through the help of others, yourself or both.

Not all gifts in life come wrapped in pretty ribbons and bows. There are many gifts you'd rather do without because they bring havoc and turmoil into your life. Yet, these presents are really opportunities that help you grow, learn, and gain insight that you may never have obtained any other way.

Make use of the dilemma you are in right now; view it from as many perspectives as you can. Then choose the route that will benefit you and others most in the long run.

Let the crazy making stay behind while you go on. It will always be there, waiting for those who want to "sign up." Start from wherever you are now, and make the very best of the moment. Make a choice or a decision that is one that moves you into a better life that truly reflects who you really are from this day forward.

SUGGESTED RESOURCES

The following resources represent a sampling of specialized workshops, therapies, tapes and other types of support for growth and healing emotionally and physically. Many people use one or more of these services alone or effectively in conjunction with general forms of counseling and therapy.

Each is unique, as are the various professionals and individuals involved in them. This list is in no way complete. Its purpose is to invite you to explore avenues you might not have known about or previously considered. Certainly you are developing your own list as life experiences, interests and needs arise.

It's truly amazing how many courses, workshops, lectures, and introductions to services are available through town and city recreation departments, human services departments and college extension courses. Utilizing these services is a good way to break out of a rut and create a higher happiness quotient.

If you are interested in learning more about the following workshops, services or audio-cassette tapes, write or call the following groups, organizations or individuals for more information. You also could ask around for local individuals and groups providing these types of services and programs that might appeal to you.

No one can fully tell you just how to get the perfect combination of services and activities for your own health and growth. You know best what is truly right for you. As a phrase from a song from Trisha Yearwood says, "You've got to listen to the whispers of your heart..." Also, the old saying, "When the student is ready, the teacher appears," certainly is appropriate too.

Here are a few of the growth and healing orientations you might consider looking into:

Cranial Sacral Emotional Release Work—For those interested in integrating touch and emotional release as a self-exploration tool.

Holotropic Breathwork —A process that combines deep breathing, evocative music and focused body work. Group and individual sessions use creative artwork and discussions to help you integrate and expand your experiences.

Reiki—A touch healing system that clears, straightens and heals energy pathways, thus allowing the life force to flow in a healthy and natural way. When a person is initiated into Reiki, she learns how to experience the healing energy that exists within as well that which is all around her. She also learns how to give a hands-on treatment to help a person's process of healing.

Structural Integration—Sat Nam Kaur Khalsa of Claremont, California, conducts structural therapy which involves structural integration. Information she provides states: "Structural Integration works the facial tissues in order to restore balance, coordination and freedom of movement. It releases chronic tension, increases flexibility, frees breathing patterns, improves posture and balances the flow of energy through the body. It has also been effective in relief of headache, back pain, constipation and menstrual problems, to name a few.

The emotional effects are often as dramatic as the changes in body structure. The results of working with the body affect the emotional, behavioral, and spiritual life of the individual."

Eye Movement Desensitization and Reprocessing (EMDR)™
EMDR is a method used to accelerate the treatment of a wide range of psychological problems related to both disturbing past events and present life conditions. It is a healing process involving self-discovery and the release of emotional and physical stress at the cellular level. For more information, call for a professional in your area who is trained to conduct EMDR.

EMDR™ Institute, INC
P.O. Box 51010
Pacific Grove, CA 93950-6010
408-372-3900

The Learning Annex

The Learning Annex
11850 Wilshire Blvd., Suite #100
Los Angeles, CA 90025
310-478-6677

This resource provides an incredible array of reasonably priced workshops and activities in the Los Angeles area and five other locations that range from self-growth and healing to business opportunity ideas and creative development.

Founded in 1981, The Learning Annex is the largest adult education organization in America. Currently schools operate in:

Los Angeles - 310-478-6677
San Francisco - 415-788-5500
San Diego - 619-544-9700
New York City - 212-570-6500
Toronto, Canada - 416-964-0011
Sacramento, California - 916-446-7070

The Center For Attention Deficit Disorders. Between 8 and 15 million people in the United States have Attention Deficit Disorder (ADD). Most of these people have no idea why they suffer from underachievement or repeated failures from various ineffective treatments. Help is available. For example, the team of professionals at the Center for Attention Deficit Disorder work to integrate ADD treatment modalitites which include assessment, medication management, diagnostic testing for learning disabilities, individual and group therapy, parent training, as well as organizational, career and educational therapies. Dr. Marilyn Kroplick, the founder of the center, is a psychiatrist and a clinical faculty member at UCLA-NPI.

Marilyn Kroplick, MD - Director
The Center for Attention Deficit Disorders
16133 Ventura Blvd., Suite 945, Encino, CA 91436
818-995-8458, (FAX) 818-995-1202

HeartWind—Laurie Weaver, founder of HeartWind, is a teacher and counselor who utilizes methods from Gestalt work, bodywork therapies and Holotropic Breathwork. She conducts workshops throughout the U.S. and abroad, exploring the combination of these modalities with creative expression through body sculpting, painting and movement. Laurie is certified in Holotropic Breathwork, having trained and apprenticed with Dr. Stanislov and Christina Grof. She has been a member of the Grof Transpersonal Training Staff. She has extensive experience working with those seeking healing of incest-related issues.

Laurie Weaver

HeartWind

250 Annis Road

Brisbane, CA 94005

415-468-6930

National Alliance for the Mentally Ill (NAMI)—NAMI is an organization which is supportive of individuals with mental illnesses and their families. Local chapters provide education, advocacy and peer support. Call the helpline at 1-800-950-NAMI.

National Alliance for the Mentally Ill (NAMI)

200 N. Glebe Road, Suite 1015

Arlington, VA 22203

703-524-7600

Helpline—1-800-950-NAMI

Helpful Tapes

"The Practice of Mindfulness in Psychotherapy I & II, " Hanh, Thich Nhat. This tape explores how to find and nourish an inner peacefulness and maintain it throughout the day.

"Why People Don't Heal" and "Energy Anatomy" tapes, Myss, Caroline. ("Energy Anatomy" is a 6-tape course.) Caroline Myss has developed a unique approach to the study of "energy anatomy"—the electromagnetic channels that connect mind and spirit, the "circuitry" crucial to the self healing process. Both available through:

Sounds True

P.O. Box 8010

Boulder, CO 80306

800-333-9185

(Call for catalog)

SUGGESTED READING

The Address Book, *7th ed.*, Michael Levine, The Berkley Publishing Group, 1995.

Are You the One for Me?, Barbara DeAngelis, Ph.D., Delacorte Press, 1992.

Choices, Mindy Bingham, Judy Edmondson and Sandy Stryker, Advocacy Press, 1989.

Coming Apart, (tapes) Daphne Rose Kingma, Sounds True Audio, 1995.

The Courage to Heal, A Guide for Survivors of Child Sexual Abuse, Ellen Bass and Laura Davis, Harper & Row, Publishers, Inc.

The Dance of Anger, Harriet Goldhor Lerner, Ph.D., Harper & Row, 1985.

Driven to Distraction, Edward M. Hallowell, M.D. and John J.Ratey, M.D., Simon & Schuster, 1994.

The Ecstatic Moment, Paul Ferrini, Heartways Press, 1996.

Flying Solo, Carol M. Anderson and Susan Stewart with Sona Dimidjian, W.W. Norton & Co., 1994.

Getting the Love You Want, Harville Hendrix, Ph.D., Harper Perrenial, 1988.

The Holotropic Mind, Stanislav Grof, M.D. with Hal Zina Bennett, Harper Collins Inc., 1993.

I Hate You—Don't Leave Me, Jerold J. Kreiseman, M.D. and Hal Straus, Avon Books, 1989.

If I Had My Life to Live Over, edited by Sandra Haldeman Martz, Papier-Mache Press, 1992

Is It Worth Dying For?, Dr. Robert S. Eliot and Dennis L. Breo, Bantam Books, 1984.

Love Without Conditions, Paul Ferrini, Heartways Press, 1994.

Man's Eternal Quest, Paramahansa Yogananda, Self-Realization Fellowship, 1975.

Men are from Mars, Women are from Venus, John Gray, Ph.D., Harper Collins, Inc., 1992.

Men Are Just Desserts, Sonja Friedman, Warner Books, 1983.

Men, Women and Relationships, John Gray, Ph.D., Beyond Words Publishing, Inc., 1993.

More Choices, Mindy Bingham and Sandy Stryker, Advocacy Press, 1987.

On Death and Dying, Elisabeth Kübler-Ross, M.D., Collier Books, Macmillan Publishing, Inc., 1970.

Overcoming Loneliness in Everyday Life, Jacqueline Olds, M.D., Richard Scwartz, M.D., and Harriet Webster, Birch Lane Press, 1996.

Owning Your Own Shadow, Robert A. Johnson, Harper Collins, 1993.

People of the Lie, M. Scott Peck, M.D., Simon & Schuster, Inc., 1983.

The Practice of Forgiveness, Lynda Bates, Copy Pro Printing, 1993.

Psycho-Cybernetics, Maxwell Maltz, M.D., F.I.C.S., Prentice-Hall, Inc., 1960.

Silence of the Heart, Paul Ferrini, Heartways Press, 1996.

Spiritual Emergency, edited by Stanislav Grof, M.D. and Christina Grof, Jeremy P. Tharcher, Inc., 1989.

The Stress Solution, Lyle H. Miller, Ph.D., Alma Dell Smith, Ph.D., with Larry Rothstein, Ed.D., Pocket Books, Simon & Schuster, Inc., 1993.

What to Do When a Parent's Love Rules Your Life, Patricia Love, Ed.D., with Jo Robinson, Bantam Books, 1990.

What Your Mother Couldn't Tell You & Your Father Didn't Know, John Gray, Ph.D., Harper Collins Publishers, Inc., 1994.

When Anger Hurts, Matthew McKay, Ph.D., Peter D. Rogers, Ph.D. and Judith McKay, R.N., New Harbinger Publications, Inc., 1989.

When Bad Things Happen to Good People, Harold H. Kushner, Avon Books, 1981.

When the Worst That Can Happen Already Has, Dennis Wholev, Hyperion, 1992.

The Wisdom of the Self, Paul Ferrini, Heartways Press, 1992.

Women with Attention Deficit Disorder, Sari Solden, MS, Underwood Books, 1995.

Woulda, Coulda Shoulda, Arthur Freeman Ph.D., and Rose DeWolf, HarperPerennial, 1989.

You Can Heal Your Life, Louise L. Hay, Hay House, Inc., 1984.

INDEX

W

Order Form

If you know of someone who would benefit from reading *What To Do When Life Is Driving You Crazy*, you can order more copies of this book by filling out the following information:

Please send_____copies of *What To Do When Life Is Driving You Crazy* to:

(Please Print)

Company:_____

Name:_____

Address:_____

City:_____State:_____Zip:_____

Please send check or money order for $14.95 plus $3.50 Priority Mail for first book; $1.00 each additional (and tax for CA orders) to:

Creative Options Publications
2058 N. Mills Avenue, Suite 116
Claremont, CA 91711
Phone: 909-624-5002   Fax: 909-624-0521

If you would like information about tapes that reinforce this book or to have Barbara Berg speak on Cognitive Stress Management at your organization or business, please call, write or fax to the above.

Order Form

If you know of someone who would benefit from reading *What To Do When Life Is Driving You Crazy*, you can order more copies of this book by filling out the following information:

Please send____copies of *What To Do When Life Is Driving You Crazy* to:

(Please Print)

Company:_____

Name:_____

Address:_____

City:_____State:_____Zip:_____

Please send check or money order for $14.95 plus $3.50 Priority Mail for first book; $1.00 each additional (and tax for CA orders) to:

Creative Options Publications
2058 N. Mills Avenue, Suite 116
Claremont, CA 91711
Phone: 909-624-5002   Fax: 909-624-0521

If you would like information about tapes that reinforce this book or to have Barbara Berg speak on Cognitive Stress Management at your organization or business, please call, write or fax to the above.